T5-AFS-430

THE
RETRANSFORMATION
OF THE
SCHOOL

Daniel Linden Duke

THE
RETRANSFORMATION
OF THE
SCHOOL

*the emergence of
contemporary alternative schools
in the United States*

NELSON-HALL/CHICAGO

To Gale Linden Duke, my mother, Paula Maguire Duke, my wife, Joshua Martin Duke, my son, and C. James Shapland, my friend . . . all of whom have served as my teachers, contributing to my own "retransformation."

Duke, Daniel Linden.
The retransformation of the school.

Bibliography: p.
Includes index.
1. Education—United States—1965-
2. Education—Experimental methods. I. Title.
LA217.D84   370'.973
ISBN 0-88229-294-3 (cloth)
ISBN 0-88229-606-X (paper)

Copyright © 1978 by Daniel Linden Duke

All rights reserved. No part of this book may be reproduced in any form without permission in writing from the publisher, except by a reviewer who wishes to quote brief passages in connection with a review written for broadcast or for inclusion in a magazine or newspaper. For information address Nelson-Hall Inc., 325 West Jackson Blvd., Chicago, Illinois 60606.

Manufactured in the United States of America

10   9   8   7   6   5   4   3   2   1

Contents

Chapter 5

SECTION II
THE ORIGINS OF CONTEMPORARY
ALTERNATIVE SCHOOLS

SECTION I

**The
Characteristics
of
Contemporary
Alternative
Schools**

1

Why Look at Contemporary Alternative Schools?

The query that serves as the title of this chapter is not totally rhetorical. Some people seriously question the need to investigate a phenomenon that accounts for little more than a handful of students, hardly a percentage point of the entire body of students presently enrolled in American elementary and secondary schools. To such an argument others respond that any challenge to the status quo, no matter how small numerically, deserves scholarly attention.

Schools are organizations. They do not exist in isolation from other organizations. When a relatively dramatic departure from conventional practice—such as the emergence of alternative schools for competent, middle-class students—occurs over a short period of time, it merits the notice of those concerned with educational change. The rise in the last decade of nonsectarian, nonmilitary, nonelitist, and noncompensatory alternative schools bespeaks tensions and discontent, not only within the sphere of education, but within the society-at-large. Who is discontented and the reasons why constitute the foci of the following study.

Historical Origins and the Significance of the Problem

The public has been barraged in the last decade with scores of terms pertaining to educational reforms. Free schools, storefront schools, continuation schools, three R's schools, magnet schools, minischools, street academies, schools-without-walls, and schools-within-schools are all part of this lexicographer's dilemma. People speak of alternative schools, alternatives to school, alternative education, and alternatives in education. Naturally, some terms carry more of a certain type of message than others. When New York's Commissioner of Education, Ewald Nyquist, felt the term "alternative school" was being linked too closely in the public mind with radical free schools, he began to speak of "optional learning environments."[1] Mario Fantini prefers "schools of choice." For the purposes of this study, however, the term "alternative school" seems most appropriate.

An alternative school simply is a school accessible by choice, not assignment. Since colonial times, alternative schools have existed in the United States. Of course, these schools have not been options for everyone or equally accessible to all groups. Most of them originally limited enrollment on the basis of religious belief, class status, or income. Several more recent varieties of alternative school have used other selection criteria.

Traditional alternative schools. These schools are nonpublic and cater to particular groups of students. Included under the heading of traditional alternatives are parochial or sectarian schools, military academies, and "prep" schools. The last two are primarily boarding schools, while parochial schools can be day or residential institutions.

A study commissioned by the National Association of

Independent Schools (N.A.I.S.) and financed by the Danforth Foundation found that, among 730 members of the N.A.I.S., coeducational day schools showed the steadiest growth. Separate-sex day schools did less well, while boarding schools and military academies were in decline.[2] While the N.A.I.S. study included very few sectarian schools, numerous reports of cutbacks and school closings by Catholic school systems seem to reflect a curtailment in the postwar growth of religious-based alternatives, at least those affiliated with Catholicism.

With the exception of the standard diocesan day school operated by the local Catholic hierarchy or the small parochial schools run by fundamentalist Protestant groups like the Amish, the traditional alternative school of recent vintage has been an option basically for upper socioeconomic groups. Sociologists such as E. Digby Baltzell, Dixon Wecter, and C. Wright Mills portray these schools as sources of cultural continuity and social credentialing for the American elite.[3] Conscious of the disadvantages of the label "elitist" in an increasingly middle-class society, many traditional alternative schools have attempted to enroll a broader cross section of the community. The N.A.I.S. report entitled *American Nonpublic Schools* can be interpreted as a specific effort to stimulate public and professional reassessment of traditional alternative schools. The author of the study somewhat apologetically cites historian James McLachlan's contention that the mission of the American boarding school "was not so much to raise up an 'aristocratic' ruling elite as to educate bourgeois gentlemen."[4] No attempt, however, is made to distinguish between "bourgeois gentlemen" and members of an "aristocratic ruling elite." The N.A.I.S. report serves as a warning to those involved in traditional alternatives that they must update their image or risk further decline.

While the forecast for many traditional alternative schools is clouded by changes in the economy and in people's attitudes toward private education, one category of traditional alternative school has experienced a significant increase. Segregationist academies have emerged throughout the United States, particularly in the South, in response to court-ordered school desegregation. One of the few researchers to investigate these new schools concludes that,

> ... the parents seem to choose a new independent school for their children for a composite of reasons rather than for a single reason. It is probable, however, that the integration of the public schools in their communities has been the catalyst in their decision making.[5]

Summerhillian alternative schools. A second type of alternative school derives its name from the well-publicized work of A. S. Neill.[6] Summerhillian alternatives are nonpublic boarding schools embracing some or all of the radical pedagogical ideas of Neill and his disciples. Often these schools are organized around communal living situations and communitarian ideals. Most schools charge tuition, which can amount to as much money as the fees charged by prestigious traditional alternatives.

Summerhillian alternative schools have existed in small numbers in the United States for several decades and include the politically-radical Macedonia community school of the fifties and bucolic Lewis-Wadhams, set up in the early sixties by Herb Snitzer. The number of Summerhillian alternatives has increased in the last ten years along with the number of contemporary alternative schools. Because the bulk of contemporary alternative schools are nonresidential and the Summerhill model predates by several decades the recent burgeoning of these schools, Summerhillian alternatives are considered a separate type of alternative school. They will not be discussed in detail in subsequent chapters.

Compensatory alternative schools. A third type of alternative school has been evolving in several forms since the development of pauper schools in the nineteenth century.[7] Compensatory alternatives are designed to supplement the work done by conventional public schools. Supported either by public or private funds, these schools, as their name suggests, seek to compensate for some "handicap" shared by their students which prevents them from succeeding in conventional learning situations. Handicaps can range from physical and mental retardation to sociopathic and delinquent behavior to "cultural disadvantagement." Students attending compensatory alternatives suffer a multitude of labels including "slow learner," "underachiever," "discipline problem," and "deprived."

Two factors must be stressed. A compensatory alternative school is not an option in exactly the same sense that Andover, Fork Union Military Academy, or the neighborhood parish school are options. Second, many reasons utilized to justify the need for compensatory education may not be recognized universally. A school for deaf students may be more defensible to some people than a special school for students from slum neighborhoods. Some blacks stress the need for separate schools within which their children can acquire the skills necessary to survive in white society. Other blacks insist that U.S. society is divided enough. They support compensatory programs *within* existing public schools.

Compensatory alternative schools encompass a wide variety of special educational programs including turn-of-the-century vocational schools designed to save impoverished youngsters from destitution and, coincidentally, to provide semiskilled labor for an industrializing nation. Special schools for the blind, deaf, mute, and those otherwise physically handicapped, correctional facilities and rehabilitation-center training programs such as those operated for drug addicts by Synanon and Phoenix House are other examples of compensatory alternatives.

Since the late fifties, a new, more controversial group of compensatory schools has emerged—schools designed to

provide minority students with a sense of racial or ethnic
identity plus a more competitive footing vis-à-vis white
middle-class students. Contrasting these street academies,
storefront schools, and black and Chicano "community
schools" with recent white free schools, Robert Barr states,

> The other group of schools, usually poor, black,
> and inner-city, might better be described as com-
> munity-control schools. Related historically to the
> earlier civil-rights freedom schools, these free
> schools typify the larger struggle of minority
> groups against racist institutions and have been
> set up by parents to liberate their children from
> the "indoctrination and destruction" of the public
> schools.[8]

Whether terms such as "culturally deprived" and "culturally disadvantaged" have theoretical legitimacy or not,
it is clear from reports by researchers like James Coleman
and Christopher Jencks that minority and lower socioeconomic class students do not profit as much from conventional public schooling as do white middle-class students.
The rise of alternatives such as Harlem Prep, Casa de la
Raza (Berkeley, California), the Albany Street Academy
(Albany, New York), and St. Michael's Community School
(Milwaukee, Wisconsin) represents a recognition of the need
to improve the prospects of poor and minority youth in
mainstream American society.

Contemporary alternative schools.   So far, three types of
alternative school have been described. None of them can be
said to cater on a nonsectarian basis to white middle-class
students of average or above average abilities—with the
possible exception of some Summerhillian boarding schools.
Since the mid-sixties, an increasing number of public and
nonpublic alternative schools fitting this description have
emerged. Due to the great diversity of names and styles
among these schools, they will be referred to simply as
"contemporary alternative schools." It is with the develop-

ment of these alternatives that the following study is concerned. What are they like and why did they appear in such relatively large numbers during the past decade?

First, contemporary alternative schools share with other alternatives the trait of accessibility by choice rather than assignment. Second, they make the pretense, at least, of a nonconventional approach to learning. This type of claim cannot be made by many other alternative schools. As Harry Broudy observes, "Historically, private schools have not been noted for either their diversity or innovation. Catholic schools certainly did not claim these virtues and until very recently did not regard them as virtues."[9] The third, and in many ways most significant, characteristic common to contemporary alternative schools is their composition. As later data indicate, these schools consist primarily of white middle-class students capable of succeeding in conventional public schools. These students do not share common ethnic, religious, social, or political backgrounds. They typically do not possess extraordinary emotional problems, though many could be described as undermotivated or discontented. While a few nonpublic alternative schools conforming to these three traits have existed previous to the recent proliferation of such schools, *public* alternative schools for competent students, outside of several in large urban areas like New York City, are virtually without precedent.

Trying to estimate accurately the number of contemporary alternative schools that have developed in the past decade is difficult, especially since the lists that exist rarely differentiate between compensatory and contemporary alternatives. A survey conducted by the newsletter "Changing Schools" found fewer than ten public alternative schools in 1964 and almost three hundred by 1972.[10] By 1975, the number of public alternative schools was reported to have risen to over a thousand, although there was evidence that the popularity of particular types of alternatives (notably schools-without-walls and open schools) had declined. Ewald Nyquist reported that the New York State Education Department estimated the existence of over a thousand public and nine hundred nonpublic alternative schools in 1973.[11] Allen Graubard, working on a federal grant to study recent nonpublic alternatives, isolated about thirty schools that existed as of 1967.[12] Several of these schools—the Peninsula School in Menlo Park, California, for example—had been started as early as the twenties. By the 1971-1972 school year, over two hundred new nonpublic alternatives had been formed, while almost two hundred more were added during the course of the next twelve months. These figures do not reflect the schools that were established and then closed before the surveys were taken. Whatever the actual number of contemporary alternative schools, it is apparent that they have exerted a profound influence on the course of American education. With encouragement from federal and state agencies, large urban and suburban school districts have moved rapidly in the direction of providing more options for students at all levels. Educators acknowledge that no one style of learning seems best for all students.

The following study is an effort to provide tentative explanations to account for the recent unparalleled emergence of contemporary alternative schools. No existing research of these schools has 1) focused primarily on their origins, 2) included both public and nonpublic alternative schools, or 3) attempted to develop in an organized manner a variety of possible explanations that, in turn, might be verified by future researchers. This study combines data from original research, primary and secondary sources dealing with recent alternatives, and secondary material on historical developments in the area of alternative schooling.

Existing literature. To date, the literature on contemporary alternative schools has been insufficient to yield a general understanding of the phenomenon. Most of the books and articles that have been written in the last ten years either deal exclusively with public alternatives or with nonpublic alternatives. The impression is created that the two have developed simultaneously, but independently.

Little hard data, other than some highly personalized accounts of the growth of particular alternative schools and some formal evaluations of federally funded public alternatives, have been collected. The best of these narratives include *The Lives of Children* by George Dennison, *Starting Your Own High School* by the Elizabeth Cleaners Street School People, and *The Teacher Was the Sea,* a description of Pacific High School by Michael Kaye. The bulk of the literature on alternatives, however, seems to be a mixture of scathing socioeducational criticism and romantic vision.

Four exceptions to these general comments are Allen Graubard's *Free the Children: Radical Reform and the Free School Movement,* Michael Katz's *Class, Bureaucracy, and Schools,* Jonathan Kozol's *Free Schools,* and Otto Kraushaar's *American Nonpublic Schools.* Graubard and Kraushaar have conducted extensive research on alternative schools, though the latter investigator limited his efforts largely to traditional alternative schools. Graubard compiled a lot of descriptive information on free schools, but did not organize it into a systematic review of these schools.

In addition, Graubard, Kozol, and Kraushaar made little attempt to explain why alternative schools emerged when they did and in such numbers. However, Kraushaar correctly observed that

> ... a ground swell of private school growth began soon after the Great Depression of the 1930s, the trend accelerated significantly after the Second World War, and crested in the midsixties. Since then, the decline in Catholic school enrollment has evidently more than offset increases in small but growing groups of Protestant and Jewish schools, black schools, segregationist academies, and experimental free community elementary schools.[13]

Kraushaar and Graubard provide highly useful de-

scriptions of particular types of contemporary and traditional alternative schools. Kozol focuses almost solely
on minority-controlled compensatory and contemporary
alternatives, though he criticizes contemporary alternatives started by middle-class whites. He is not certain
whether young, socially-aware whites should concentrate
their efforts on the development of alternative schools for
underprivileged minority students or forget their preten-
sions about being "involved" and accept their "middle-
classness." In any event, Kozol displays little tolerance for
alternative schools catering to competent, economically
well-off students.

Kozol, Katz, and, to a lesser extent Graubard, share a
Marxian perspective on social change. Only Katz presents
a well-reasoned historical argument to suggest that public
education in the United States is more the triumph of class
interests than the premeditated salvation of the masses.
Aside from his final chapter, Katz focuses exclusively on
educational reform in the nineteenth century and the reasons why public schools adopted the bureaucratic mode
of organization. Though he avoids a "conspiracy theory"
of American public education, he also rejects the notion
that the choice of a bureaucratic structure for public
schools was purely accidental. His concluding chapter is a
provocative application of his thesis to current educational
developments, including the growth of alternative schools.

The criticism of the works of Graubard, Katz, Kozol,
and Kraushaar is not intended to detract from these
writers' efforts to increase public awareness of the phenomenon of alternative schooling. Each has provided assistance
to the student of contemporary alternative schools. Having
read their books and the other available literature, though,
one is left with uncertainties concerning the development of
these schools. Have traditional sources of educational innovations been instrumental in the rise of alternatives? Are
new factors present? Is the author of a *Time* article correct
when he contends that free schools "are motivated less by

ideology than by despair with public education"?[14] This kind of simplistic description of the origins of recent alternatives has contributed to the erroneous impression that one or two factors can explain the emergence of hundreds of public and nonpublic alternative schools.

A further shortcoming of the literature is the failure to define the separate motives guiding parent, student, and teacher support of alternative schools. Educators may be interested in alternatives for reasons quite distinct from those accounting for parental involvement. Recent observers simply have failed to appreciate the diversity of reasons for creating and supporting contemporary alternative schools.

Attacking the Problem—Research Procedures

Before alternative schools can be explained, they must be described. Without a systematic description of contemporary alternatives, it would be difficult to understand whether the subject at hand represented a diverse body of educational experiments sharing only their common opposition to conventional schooling or a relatively homogeneous group of schools striving to address similar problems with similar programs. Should the descriptive phase of the study point to the existence of particular traits common to many or most alternative schools, it would serve as the basis for further investigation and, possibly, the discovery of unanticipated explanatory factors. For example, nowhere in the literature on alternatives is mention made of the role played by single parents in setting up and supporting alternative schools. In collecting descriptive data on the composition of these schools, however, it was discovered that the parent groups supporting many schools are composed of large numbers of single parents. Further probing revealed the fact that some alternative schools have received impetus from groups of single parents in need of affiliation and involvement with people sharing similar concerns.

Chapters 2 through 5 are devoted to a description of contemporary alternative schools based on the author's own research plus the small corpus of existing information. No pretense is made that the new research meets the most rigorous demands of quantitative analysis. To have collected data from so many schools (40) and still observed all the conventions of statistical validity and reliability would have been impossible, given the objectives of the study (to develop tentative explanations) and the resources available to the author. Rather than the establishment of proof that one or two factors definitely influenced the emergence of contemporary alternatives, the ultimate purpose of the study was to bring a degree of orderliness to a wide-open, previously unresearched area.

In an effort to fortify the contention that contemporary alternative schools are without extensive precedent and to enhance the descriptive section of the study, data concerning earlier alternative schools and educational innovations is introduced periodically. Much of the historical data herein is the product of revisionist historians.[15] The iconoclastic spirit pervading recent writing in the field of educational history has tended to expose the "myth" of American public schooling, namely that the public school was designed with the best interests of an egalitarian society in mind. Drawing from new works by scholars such as Joseph Cronin, Michael Katz, and Joel Spring, along with older works by Lawrence Cremin and James McLachlan, the author hopes to create a historical context for the emergence of contemporary alternatives.

The sample. To provide a data base from which to derive generalizations concerning the characteristics of contemporary alternative schools, a sample of forty alternative schools was selected randomly from a population of 253 schools. No comprehensive listing of all public and non-public alternative schools has been published; thus, estimating the total number of schools from which to draw the sample was difficult. A population was fashioned from several sources, including a list of sixty public school districts experimenting with alternatives that appeared in *Nation's Schools* and a directory of nonpublic alternatives completed by Allen Graubard.[16] For reasons of research feasibility (since each of the forty schools in the sample had to be visited for at least a day), the sample was drawn from alternatives located east of the Mississippi River.[17] It is the author's opinion that the final list of 253 schools represented a major portion of the actively functioning contemporary alternative schools in the eastern half of the United States during the 1972-1973 school year. Any schools that were excluded simply were not mentioned in the literature or included on any published listing.

Because contemporary alternative schools cut across age lines, the sample was divided into three parts: schools for children ages three or four to thirteen, schools for adolescents thirteen to eighteen, and schools including both, or portions of both, groups. Dividing the population and the sample by age level was a precaution based on the possibility that elementary alternatives, for example, developed for reasons different from those accounting for secondary alternatives. For the same reason, the sample was divided between public and nonpublic alternatives.

The chart below shows the number sampled from each group and the total population size in parentheses. There were too few combined elementary-secondary public alternatives to merit investigation. Approximately one-sixth of each population group was selected, thus yielding a sample size of forty schools. A simple mixing drum technique was employed to assure a basically random sample.

CONTEMPORARY ALTERNATIVE SCHOOLS SAMPLE[18]

	Elementary	Secondary	Combined
Nonpublic Alternatives	15 (93)	6 (40)	8 (53)
Public Alternatives	5 (29)	6 (38)	

Observation. In order to facilitate on-the-spot collection of descriptive data, the author initially modified an observation schedule used in a previous study of open education in New York State.[19] Four alternative schools were visited, extensive notes taken, and the observation schedule used. From the notes and schedule data were gathered seventy-two characteristics that might describe the curriculum, instruction, and administration of an innovative school. These items were arranged in the form of a checklist, and a four-question interview schedule dealing with the origins and philosophy of the school was appended. This instrument was pilot-tested in four new alternative schools.

It was found that the instrument was more of a liability than an asset. The seventy-two item checklist tended to pick up useless data. Some of the items presumed an arbitrary distinction between subjects like curriculum content and decision-making structure. Several times, for instance, the author found that the school's organization *was* the curriculum. What seemed to be needed was an instrument that might detect broad areas of similarity between alternative schools of a specific type.

Since contemporary alternative schools are a relatively recent phenomenon, there are few, if any, "experts" in the field. As a result, it was impossible to rely on the judgment of a group of scholars to validate an instrument capable of picking up general patterns of organizational structure, methods, and instrumental influences. Of the people writing about alternative schools there are few who agree on which aspects of alternatives are more important than others. Michael Katz and Robert Riordan see the organizational structure of these schools as critical.[20] Allen Graubard and Jonathan Kozol stress the nature of the school community, particularly its socioeconomic composition.[21] Richard Saxe and Gordon Van Hooft, among others, feel the true essence of contemporary alternatives resides in their daily operations—the ways in which students are organized, time and space allocated, and resources utilized.[22] With such diversity of opinion, it was necessary to adopt a highly generalized set of observational categories from the work of Harold J. Leavitt. Leavitt is concerned with the broad characteristics of organizational change rather than change within any specific type of organization (i.e., a school).

Leavitt suggests looking at organizations in terms of their (1) objectives (tasks), (2) methods (technology), (3) administrative or decision-making organization (structure), and (4) composition (members).[23] These four categories were taken and interpreted in terms appropriate to schools. Organizational objectives became educational goals and philosophy. Methods or technology were equated with instruction, curriculum organization, and evaluation. Administrative organization or structure was taken to represent the people who made decisions in the school and the procedures by which those decisions were made. Composition pertained to the parents, students, teachers, and administrators involved in the school.

Since Leavitt does not deal specifically with the impetuses to organizational development and change, it was necessary to add a fifth category to his quartet. This category covered the reasons why people connected with alternatives felt the schools had been created in the first place.

With these five categories and data from previous experiences visiting alternatives, on-site interviews were conducted and observations recorded at eight previously unvisited alternative schools. Notes were taken and people asked to evaluate the usefulness of the five broad areas of investigation. What resulted was a more polished instrument containing the five basic categories, each of which had been broken down into subcategories. The subcategories covered items that were found in at least one of the eight pilot-tested schools—in other words, items that might be anticipated to exist in some alternatives. This final set of items was arranged in the form of an interview schedule and pilot-tested in four additional schools.[24] In only one instance was it necessary to add another subcategory. Consequently, the items in the interview schedule seemed appropriate for the task of gathering descriptive data in a relatively systematic fashion.

Visiting each of forty schools for one or two days limits, to a certain extent, the comprehensivenes of the descriptive survey. Little agreement, however, exists concerning the most appropriate length of time for an on-site visitation. In a typical visit, the author would arrive at a school around eight in the morning and tour the facilities. During the course of the day he would converse at length with at least two teachers and, when available, two parents. In secondary schools, two or more students also would be interviewed. Visits frequently extended beyond the school day as invitations were extended by teachers or parents for evening meals and lodging. In several instances, the author actually taught a class or two. Where interview and observation data conflicted or were incomplete, follow-up inquiries by mail were made.

An appropriate time to study new schools? The argument can be made that efforts to explain specific events must be postponed until a sufficient amount of time has elapsed to ensure objectivity. No one is quite certain what a "sufficient" length of time is, however. In the case of contemporary alternative schools, the author felt that postponing study of these schools would risk the loss of much data and sacrifice ecological validity. Few individuals actively involved in the establishment of alternatives have taken the time to record their beginnings. Hundreds, if not thousands, of schools have opened and closed already without any formal record being taken. The "spirit of the sixties," a difficult-to-define entity at best, apparently has dissipated. The more removed the researcher becomes from the period in question, the greater the possibility of misinterpretation or misunderstanding.

The author feels his personal involvement in the establishment and operation of a contemporary alternative school has been more a research asset than a liability. The study, however, is not an attempt to support or to condemn alternatives. The author's personal contact with alternative schools has served only to sensitize him to certain aspects of these schools.

Schools are not apart from society. A tendency persists in some educational research to isolate schools from society at large. Innovations like open education and slogans such as "relevance" and "humanistic education" are discussed without more than a superficial effort being made to relate them to community or national developments. Anthony Oettinger cautions that schools, as institutions, are intertwined with all other institutions. He observes:

> Changing school hours affects not only pupils and school personnel but every mother as well. Introducing the "new math" shakes up every parent in town. Attempting administrative decentralization stirs storms of union protests. Ability grouping invites federal court decisions prohibiting it. If part of the high school burns down, it is cheaper for taxpayers in some localities to build a new one because the state contributes to new construction but not to renovation. An experiment with a new high school curriculum raises the specter of low performance on College Boards. And, most obvious, the people who make up every other institution, from the family to the Presidency, are products of the schools.[25]

Phrased somewhat differently, the same idea is expressed by Allen Graubard when he argues that "the real problems of educational reform are social, political, economic, and ideological."[26]

In addition to being guilty of the institutional isolation of schools from the mainstream of American society, many educational researchers have treated all schools as if they conformed to the model of a conventional public school. The literature contains few references to public and nonpublic alternative schools, be they traditional, Summerhillian, compensatory, or contemporary.

To broaden the perspective of educational research, it is important to consider the theories and concepts of scholars in other fields. The historian, for one, can offer great insight into the matter of educational change, as Lawrence Cremin demonstrates in *The Transformation of the School.* Care must be taken, though, to avoid the historian's common error of seeing every event in terms of a seemingly endless succession of precedents.

An investigation into the origins of contemporary alternative schools can benefit from several social science techniques and concepts. Sociohistorical trend analysis and organizational theory are but two examples.

Combing historical material for the appearance of trends is a practice almost as old as the study of history itself.[27] During the past fifty years, sociologists have adopted the study of trends and given it a more quantitative character. Complex statistical formulas are employed to compare such things as suicide rates with political or economic trends. For the purposes of this study, a less sophisticated approach to trend analysis will be taken. The work of two social scientists, Otto Kraushaar and Joel Spring, illustrates the contribution an awareness of trends can make to the study of school reform.

Writing about the discontent muckrakers voiced over public education in the twenties, Spring comments:

> The discontent with the schools ranged from radical anarchists to some union groups. The result was an attempt to establish alternative systems of education. Before and after World War I discontent with the industrial domination of the schools bred a series of experimental schools designed as models to counteract the reactionary nature of the public schools. The search for

alternative forms of education to the public school was to become one of the important strands of educational development in the twentieth century.[28]

Kraushaar writes of more recent trends in alternative schooling:

> Overall, the schools of the NAIS group show in recent years a slow but steady growth, but at a rate slower than that of the public schools. It suggests that costly elite schooling is in relatively lower demand than five years ago. . . .
>
> Another sector of private education experiencing a ferment of growth is the group of new, "free" or community schools which are sprouting up in major population centers from coast to coast.[29]

Pointing to the evolution of alternatives over the past three or four decades is one way to approach a discussion of the factors influencing the growth of contemporary alternative schools. A later chapter will discuss, for example, the influence of rising birth rates after World War II on the emergence of these schools.

Theories of organizational change and concepts pertaining to the structure of organizations can be borrowed from the fields of sociology and educational administration and applied to the study of alternative schools. The use of Harold Leavitt's model in the development of an interview schedule is just one example. Warren Bennis, Amitai Etzioni, and Matthew Miles have written extensively about the growth of new organizations and the factors influencing their development.[30] Arguing that an understanding of organizations is critical to an understanding of historical events, Michael Katz writes that organization

> . . . was the medium through which groups or classes organized their response to social imperatives. In short, organization mediated between social change and social structure. Hence men brought to the design of their organizations their

values, their ambivalences, their fears, and, above all, their aspirations for the shape of American society.[31]

This kind of observation, so prevalent in recent literature on the growth of American education, led the author to spend considerable time investigating the structure of alternative schools. It was simply impossible to gain a full understanding of these schools through a study of their pedagogical characteristics alone.

There are, no doubt, other borrowings that might shed as much light on contemporary alternatives as those from the fields of historical research, educational administration, and sociology. Rosabeth Moss Kanter has pointed to the possibilities for greater understanding of communal alternatives through social psychological investigation. In conjunction with the recent revival of utopian communities among the young, she speaks of an American "propensity for forming voluntary associations."[32] If such a propensity actually characterizes American behavior, it might have influenced the growth of contemporary alternative schools. Presently, however, the concept is ill-defined and difficult to measure. In the future, the social psychologist along with the anthropologist and the political scientist might be able to contribute greatly to an understanding of the educational change process.

Organization of This Study

The study is divided into two sections; the first deals with description and the second concerns the presentation of tentative explanations. Chapters 2 through 5 are concerned with describing the goals, pedagogical dimensions, administrative organization, and composition of contemporary alternative schools. An effort is made in each chapter to develop generalizations characterizing most of the schools in the sample. These generalizations, in turn, are used to suggest possible factors accounting for the emergence of contemporary alternatives in the late sixties and early seventies.

The second section of the study consists of four chapters dealing with the origins of contemporary alternatives and a concluding chapter summarizing the study's findings and their significance. An attempt is made to arrange the various impetuses in an orderly, meaningful fashion. This task is accomplished by distinguishing between impetuses from top-level sources such as government agencies, universities, and school administrators and impetuses from grassroots sources such as parents, students, and individual teachers.

The final chapters essentially address a single question. When popular discontent with education has existed in various forms for decades, why should the United States have experienced the rapid growth of contemporary alternative schools only in the past decade?

The last half of the study ultimately demonstrates that a number of factors converged during the sixties to stimulate the development of alternatives for competent middle-class students. No single or simple explanation, as some have suggested, will suffice to explain the proliferation of these schools.

2

Contemporary Alternative Schools: Their Goals

It is reasonable to expect that information concerning the expressed goals of contemporary alternative schools can shed light on their origins. A second expectation is that no single goal characterizes all alternative schools. Just as there is no single type of middle-class family or competent student, there is no predominant set of common purposes guiding each of the hundreds of alternatives that have emerged since the mid-sixties.

The literature on recent alternatives portrays a variety of goals. Allen Graubard finds the concept of freedom central to the thinking of most people involved in nonpublic "free schools." In addition, he distinguishes between four types of free school:

1. The classical free school based on the Summerhill model.
2. The parent-teacher cooperative elementary

school, populated largely by young, white,
liberal, middle-class families and characterized
by a significant amount of parental input into
the decision-making process.
3. The free high school—actually a broad category
including white, working class high schools for
"drop-outs" and "push-outs," street academies
for poor minority youth, and small high schools
for relatively radical white students of average
or above average means.
4. Community elementary schools controlled by
dissatisfied, usually minority, parent groups
and characterized by a somewhat conservative
curriculum.[1]

The major problem with Graubard's typology is its
lack of consistent criteria. For certain free schools,
the distinguishing factor seems to be socioeconomic composition. For other types, the governing structure, grade
level, or philosophy constitutes the basis for grouping.
The category "free high school" is so broad it can be
broken up into three distinct types. Though a useful tool,
Graubard's typology does not differentiate between goals,
methods, and administrative organization existing in contemporary alternative schools.

Bruce Cooper identifies six alternative school models:
1. parent-teacher cooperative school
2. community freedom school
3. therapeutic school
4. free high school
5. public alternative school
6. residential free school.[2]

Cooper uses administrative organization as a grouping
criterion in one, five, and six. In four he uses grade level.
In two and three the criterion is the goal of the school.
Number five encompasses various criteria, though the distinguishing trait seems to be its "public" status.

To understand the diversity of traits subsumed under

the rubric of the contemporary alternative school, two distinct sets of criteria are necessary; i.e., the primary goal of the school, and the type of administrative organization employed. No single type of goal corresponds exclusively to any particular organizational type. This fact reinforces the belief that contemporary alternative schools are complex phenomena deriving from various impetuses. No single explanation suffices to account for their emergence.

Types of Educational Goals

Classifying alternative schools according to their avowed purposes is not a simple procedure. A rough idea of the various goals to expect can be obtained from the current books and articles dealing with educational change. Most of the alternative schools designated one or two goals from among this assortment to be of primary importance. A few schools, however, demonstrated uncertainty concerning their ultimate purpose.

Whether the schools in the sample actually were achieving the goal or goals they espoused could not be determined. This subject might be the basis for future research. The following seven configurations of goals represent "intended" goals. They were found in the written statements of purpose drafted by many schools and in interviews with parents, teachers, and students. The wide variety of goals indicates that contemporary alternative schools do not embody any one ideology or approach to learning.

Exploratory goals. Providing students with extensive amounts of unscheduled time and freedom to pursue their own interests is the essence of exploratory goals. Activities directed by adults are minimized. Student-initiated projects abound. Terms characterizing schools that espouse exploratory goals include "British infant school model," "open education," and "integrated day." Some alternative schools permit almost all activities to be student-initiated, while others establish certain basic requirements, typically in reading and mathematics. Generally, specific objectives of "exploratory" schools include creativity, natural growth, the development of individual interests, and respect for individual differences.

Preparatory goals. Alternative schools seeking preparatory goals strive to ready students for relatively specific, socially acceptable occupations. "Career education," training, and individualized instruction often characterize the academic program which is preparatory. Admission to college or satisfactory employment are two of the most common preparatory objectives. Many conventional public schools, as well as some contemporary and most compensatory schools, espouse preparatory goals.

The difference between a contemporary alternative school with preparatory goals and a compensatory alternative school with preparatory goals are not always obvious. The distinction seems to center on the capabilities of the students. If the school enrolls basically competent and motivated students, as does Washington's public School Without Walls or New York's nonpublic Harlem Prep, it can be said to be a contemporary alternative with preparatory goals. Berkeley College Preparatory in California is another example of such a school. A brochure on the school describes its goals thusly:

> Purpose of the program is to build college survival skills for youths who might otherwise not have gained the academic background for advanced studies. A course by that name—College Survival Skills—is required of all eleventh graders. Tenth graders take U. S. History. Both take math and English, with stress on building up reading skills.[3]

If the school caters to "drop-outs," "push-outs," or students with marked learning disabilities, such as the nonpublic Christian Action Ministry (C.A.M.) Academy in Chicago or the public Bennington Program in Vermont, it can be termed a compensatory alternative school with preparatory goals. College admission is rarely, if ever, the target for these schools. The basic objectives are usually gainful employment and social adjustment.

Revolutionary goals. Alternative schools advocating preparatory goals and those espousing revolutionary goals both seek to "prepare" students. The former prepare them for socially acceptable occupations. The latter, however, prepare students for lives that are not respected or supported by "mainstream" America. Alternative schools that attempt to stimulate "third world consciousness," to introduce various countercultural practices and conceptions of morality, or to encourage radical social and political activism evidence revolutionary goals. These goals can be found in the philosophical statements advanced by many commune-based schools. Schools modeled after Summerhill, though often organized communally, are noticeably apolitical, however. Where revolutionary goals are politicized, they tend to be aligned to ideologies that oppose corporate capitalism and "big government." Some of the most common features of "revolutionary" schools are their efforts to provide learning materials that are free of racial, sexist, and class biases.

Participatory goals. These goals embody a firm belief in democratic processes, specifically where students and parents, as well as teachers, participate in the governance and administration of the school. The New England town meeting often is adopted as a model. Stress is placed on learning to act responsibly through the actual exercise of decision-making responsibility. Student government, unlike that found in conventional public schools, is invested with real power. A sense of "community" is sought. Often, alternative schools with participatory goals express their curricula in terms of the operation of the schools themselves.

Therapeutic goals. The school that strives to achieve therapeutic goals does not necessarily enroll students with severe emotional or learning problems. Therapeutic goals are construed to pertain to the processes by which individuals learn about themselves, their feelings, and the way they react to others. While participatory goals focus on the group and the community, therapeutic goals center on the individual student. Considerable time is devoted to introspection, values clarification, and exploratory "rap" sessions.

Academic goals. While therapeutic goals concern affective growth, academic goals are cognitive in emphasis. Unlike exploratory goals that presume a significant amount of student-initiated activity, academic goals are based on the belief that students cannot make intelligent choices in life unless they are exposed to a broad variety of learning experiences. This exposure often requires adult intervention. Courses and other learning opportunities are provided, not only in standard curricular areas, but in less generalized fields such as ecology, comparative religions, revolutionary history, and Afro-American literature. Programs for the highly motivated or the gifted student typically embrace academic goals. Students may participate in interdisciplinary courses, in-depth courses of college caliber, seminars, field trips, and sophisticated research projects.

Demonstrative goals. While concerned with students and learning, demonstrative goals stress the "lighthouse" function of the school. In other words, the alternative school exists as a demonstration center illustrating a particular approach to education. The expectation underlying demonstrative goals is that professionals and lay alike will visit the school and proliferate information about what they witness.

A note on the "conventional public school." Throughout this study the term "conventional public school" is

used. Its use is not intended to denote that all nonalternative
schools are absolutely identical. As Harry Broudy cautions,

> We do not have national textbooks, and in many
> states there are no prescribed state texts. There is
> no national curriculum, no national system of
> teacher certification--indeed, as I have pointed out
> repeatedly, there is not even the semblance of con-
> sensus on what quality in schooling or teaching
> should mean.[4]

Despite Broudy's argument, though, public schools do
share many basic similarities. Regarding goals, they
generally espouse a variety of purposes while, in reality,
stressing those of a preparatory nature. Some revisionist
historians such as Joel Spring go as far as to argue that
all the "public schools of the twentieth century were
organized to meet the needs of the corporate state and
consequently, to protect the interests of the ruling elite
and the technological machine."[5]

The administrative organization of public schools
typically resembles the bureaucratic model, a fact to be
discussed at length in Chapter 4. Further indications that
the references to "conventional public schools" have validity are based on the impact of federal aid to education,
modern textbook production, standardized testing, and
college admissions requirements. These factors all contribute to considerable standardization of curriculum. In
addition, the process by which teachers are trained does
not vary significantly from state to state. In an age of
increasing transience, regionalization, administrative centralization, and standardization, it is naive to contend that
the multibillion dollar public education business has not undergone extensive "conventionalization."

The Goals of Contemporary Alternative Schools

Few schools can be characterized by a single educational goal. The majority of schools visited by the author
encompassed several goals. These were usually easy to

identify. For example, in a statement from its brochure, the Community School in Salem, Virginia, clearly demonstrated that exploratory goals were important:

> The major objective of the school is to give the responsibility of freedom to the student. In this sense, it is their school. When they are required to face their own needs, they begin to discipline themselves. . . . The job of the teacher at Community School is to encourage and inform the student of the usefulness of the humanities, arts, sciences and practical crafts in the curriculum without killing the natural curiosity all children are born with.

The chart below presents the predominant goals of the sampled alternative schools. Some schools embodied one set of goals, others several sets, and still others no clear goals at all. Goals naturally can change as a school develops. The chart represents the goal or goals at the time the school was established. With surprisingly few exceptions, though, the original goal or goals tended to remain constant over time. Dramatic shifts in goals were the exception rather than the rule.

A survey of the data reveals that exploratory, preparatory, and academic goals exist in the greatest frequencies. Certain types of school are characterized more by certain goals than by others. As might be expected, no public school espouses revolutionary goals. All five public elementary alternatives, however, embody demonstrative goals. Because of the general immaturity of the students, elementary schools do not stress academic or participatory goals.

First, many alternative schools manifest a blatant rejection of the pedagogical traits perceived to exist in conventional public schools. The prevalence of exploratory and academic goals among both public and nonpublic alternative schools reflects discontent with standard curricular offerings, instructional techniques, and methods of student evaluation.

Table 1

THE GOALS OF CONTEMPORARY ALTERNATIVE SCHOOLS*

Goals	Public Elementary (5)	Nonpublic Elementary (15)	Public Secondary (6)	Nonpublic Secondary (6)	Nonpublic Combined (8)
Exploratory	2	9	2	1	4 = 18
Preparatory	1	5	2	1	3 = 12
Revolutionary	0	6	0	0	1 = 7
Participatory	0	0	1	3	1 = 5
Therapeutic	0	1	0	1	0 = 2
Academic	0	1	4	4	2 = 11
Demonstrative	5	0	0	0	1 = 6
No clear-out goals	0	4	0	0	1 = 5

*Though forty schools were sampled, some schools were entered under several categories of goals. Thus there are more than forty tallies.

Second, not all alternative schools reject the typical view of schooling as preparation for the future. Twelve of the forty schools stress relatively conventional preparatory goals, including "the three R's," vocational training, and college admission.

Third, despite the emphasis on radical themes in much of the popular literature dealing with alternative education, few of the schools in the sample are characterized by revolutionary goals. Jonathan Kozol observes that more writers mention Bill Ayers' radical free school in Ann Arbor, Michigan, which lasted only a few years, than cite Edward Carpenter's highly successful Harlem Prep.[6] It is interesting to note that of the six nonpublic alternative schools advocating revolutionary goals at the time of their inception, only two continued to promote radical themes. The extent of revolutionary objectives in most contemporary alternative schools is limited to the desire to stimulate nonracist, nonsexist, and nonclassist attitudes and to encourage a general awareness of alternative lifestyles. Allen Graubard concludes,

The great majority of [free] schools have no

clear political doctrine and do not present themselves as espousing any particular political line.
On the other hand, many people involved as teachers and organizers are quite openly political, often
with experience in the civil rights, student, and
antiwar movements.[7]

Fourth, contrary to the skepticism of many observers,
most contemporary alternative schools possess a reasoned
philosophy or set of objectives. Only five of the forty
schools in the sample lacked any semblance of consistent
goals. One of the serendipitous by-products of the growth of
alternative schools may be an increased tendency for those
involved in educational innovation to articulate their goals.

Fifth, contemporary alternative schools cannot be
characterized by any particular type of goal. Their diversity of objectives suggests that no one factor is responsible
for their growth.

Historical Antecedents

It is fashionable to claim that an unorthodox or innovative undertaking is unparalleled in history. Much of
the rhetoric of the sixties embodied this kind of naive
ignorance of the past. Some researchers now acknowledge
that many facets of the recent "revolution" were echoes of
the efforts of earlier activists. Writing about the current
wave of communal experiments, sociologist Rosabeth Moss
Kanter concludes that every type of present-day commune
existed in the nineteenth century.[8] Though alternative
schools for competent, middle-class students have never
existed in such profusion, they, too, have precedents.
Similarly, educational history records examples of schools
embracing each of the seven goals characterizing contemporary alternative schools.

Alternatives embracing exploratory goals have existed
in the United States at least since the disciples of Friedrich
Froebel began establishing kindergartens and day schools
in the late nineteenth century. Some of the experimental

schools of the early twentieth century can be described as exploratory too. New York City's Children's School, established by Margaret Naumburg in 1914, typifies this group. The purpose of the school was to help children "create their own type of environment, as a direct outgrowth of their spontaneous needs and interests."[9] The school accommodated around thirty students ranging in age from two to seven. The curriculum of the Children's School "would have to be subordinated and even sacrificed temporarily if need be to the personal problem of each child."[10]

Preparatory goals have been a dimension of schooling in the United States since colonial times. Girls received one kind of education designed to prepare them for subservient, domesticated roles in society. Boys received preparatory training based on their socioeconomic status. The most blatantly preparatory schools were probably the pauper schools. By the mid-nineteenth century these schools were providing instruction that guaranteed "the working class would be alert, obedient, and so thoroughly attuned to discipline through group sanctions that a minimum of policing would ensure the preservation of social order."[11] At the other end of the social spectrum, elitist "prep" schools such as Andover, Exeter, and the "St. Grottlesex" group turned out the leaders of American business and government. Military academies such as Fork Union and Staunton trained the boys who would become officers in the armed services.

Revolutionary goals have been sought by alternative schools at various times during the development of this country. The utopian movements of the nineteenth century fostered a handful of commune-based schools, including the one founded by Robert Owen, William Maclure, and other intellectuals at New Harmony, Indiana. Maclure hoped to establish "a Pestalozzian school system to educate the children of these utopias."[12] In 1907 Marietta Johnson established her famous Organic School in Fairhope, Alabama, site of a community developed by single-tax disciples of Henry George. She strove to amalgamate progressive educational theory with radical social ideas.[13] Other schools pursuing revolutionary goals included the Modern School, formed in 1910 by a group of New York City "anarchists, socialists, single taxers, and free thinkers" and Manumit, a boarding school set up in 1924 for the children of workers.[14]

Participatory goals have been the hallmark of most American attempts to establish Summerhillian alternative schools. Even before the community-centered educational ideas of A. S. Neill reached the United States, however, there were schools stressing the importance of student responsibility and decision-making. Founded in 1915, the Stony Ford School in Stony Ford, New York, epitomized these beliefs. Designed for students up to the age of fourteen, the school was based on the feeling that adult and student members of the school community should enjoy the same social rights and obligations. As the school's attitude toward the child was described in 1917,

> He is some day to become part of the great community, the world, and he can best be fitted to be a responsible unit in it by first becoming part of a smaller community which he can understand. Responsibility, like other qualities, can best be developed by its exercise. Practically the whole management of the school is shared in by the children. . . .[15]

Just as there presently are few contemporary alternatives stressing therapeutic goals, there have not existed many in the past. The schools identifying with the pedagogical theory of Rudolf Steiner are exceptions. Embodying an approach to learning based on a naturalistic view of the child, a handful of American schools appeared in the twenties along the lines developed in Steiner's Waldorf School in Stuttgart, Germany. Steiner's philosophy was based on the need "to counterbalance the materialistic conceptions of science by a pedagogy that stresses the child's encounter of the world with his whole being—his mind, his heart and his will."[16] Many alternatives have incorporated aspects of therapeutic goals, while stopping short of structuring their entire approach upon the "exploration of self." Traditional "prep" schools encouraged the growth of "character," parochial schools the nurturance of morality, and progressive schools the cultivation of individual differences.

Academic goals can be traced to the Latin grammar schools and academies that appeared from colonial times through the antebellum era. The more illustrious nonpublic "prep" schools sought to provide a strong foundation for budding scholars. So, too, did a few public specialty schools in large urban areas. Bronx Science is one such public school, and it boasts an impressive list of internationally known graduates.

Alternative schools that attempted to serve as demonstration centers date back at least to 1896 and the establishment at the University of Chicago of the Laboratory School (later known as the Dewey School after its first administrator).[17] Other "lab," "experimental," and "lighthouse" schools followed, including the Lincoln School at Teachers College and the Milne School in Albany, New York. These schools existed ostensibly as centers where educators, teachers-in-training, and nonprofessionals could observe new instructional methods and organizational techniques in operation. Some of these schools tended, however, to become exclusive nonpublic schools for the children of professors and leading local citizens.

Conclusion

Historically, alternative schools embraced goals as diverse as those of contemporary alternatives. The absence of any one predominant goal seems to suggest that no single factor can account for the development of recent alternatives or those in earlier years. The goals established by previous alternatives were motivated by factors as diverse as the utopian movements of the nineteenth century, the rise of populism and progressivism, the adoption of a "scientific approach" to teaching, and radical sociopolitical critiques. The various goals espoused by contemporary alternatives bespeak an equally wide variety of influences. Schools with academic, preparatory, therapeutic, and demonstrative goals derive in part from a popular rejection of certain aspects of conventional schooling. Schools with exploratory, participatory, and revolutionary goals derive from criticisms, not only of public education, but of American society in general. Participatory and revolutionary goals bespeak feelings of powerlessness and discontent with the manner in which schools traditionally have been administered. Exploratory and therapeutic goals represent a reaction to prevailing attitudes toward childrearing and discipline.

Contemporary alternative schools, as a complex group of phenomena, defy labels such as "radical" or "experimental." The pursuit of participatory and academic goals by many alternatives reflects relatively conservative values. Preparatory goals typically focus on socially acceptable careers. In addition, the fact that a number of alternatives embody several distinct goals suggests, as has Philip Slater, that many Americans are ambivalent about the matter of goals. Slater contends that Americans have been unable to resolve successfully the need for security and the desire for risk and adventure.[18] Stated in another way, the society has not demonstrated a clear mandate in favor of either community or individuality.

Contemporary alternative schools cannot be explained simply as a recent manifestation of traditional American ambivalence over goals, though. Despite historical examples of alternatives with contemporary goals, there is no significant precedent for the composition of recent alternative schools. Many of the historical examples cited earlier were composed of working-class, upper-class, or disadvantaged students. Where alternative schools for capable, middle-class students did exist, they were isolated ventures, hardly comparable to the hundreds of contemporary alternative schools that have emerged in the last decade.

3

Contemporary Alternative Schools: Their Methods

Data concerning the goals of contemporary alternative schools shed some light on their possible origins. What clues can be gathered from a review of the instructional methods and other pedagogical dimensions characterizing these schools?

Ways of Grouping Students

Students can be grouped in three ways, by age, ability, and type of instruction. Age-wise, students can be grouped according to grade level (where each grade roughly corresponds to a chronological year), or in family or mixed-age groups (where two or three grades are combined), or in no specific format (as in the case of a one-room schoolhouse enrolling students in grades K-12). Most conventional public schools opt for the first type of age-grouping. The following chart depicts age-grouping in the sample.

Table 2
AGE-GROUPING IN CONTEMPORARY ALTERNATIVE SCHOOLS

Age Groups	Public Elementary (5)	Nonpublic Elementary (15)	Public Secondary (6)	Nonpublic Secondary (6)	Nonpublic Combined (8)
Grades	1	0	1	0	0 = 2
Mixed-Age Units	4	8	1	0	3 = 16
No Format	0	7	4	6	5 = 22

In most instances the innovative mixed-age group or completely nonage-grouped format is preferred. Various combinations have been attempted. The public St. Paul Open School and nonpublic Warehouse Cooperative School in Roxbury, Massachusetts, utilize a fully mixed K-12 program. Many nonpublic alternative elementary schools also include a preschool or day-care component. Some observers see this tendency to create learning groups of wider age spans as an effort to recapture the intimacy and cooperation of the traditional one-room schoolhouse. Others simply find that breaking down grade barriers encourages continuous student progress. Some conventional public schools, particularly elementary schools attracted to the British infant school model, also have begun to experiment with mixed-age grouping. The trend is not limited to contemporary alternatives.

Grouping by ability is another possibility, one which currently is regarded with some lack of popularity. At least one court case (in Washington, D.C.) has declared the practice of homogeneous or ability-grouping in public schools unconstitutional. Schools have experimented with various types of homogeneous and heterogeneous mixing, though research findings generally do not support any method more than another.[1] Three basic categories of ability-grouping exist: completely heterogeneous grouping, limited homogeneous grouping in reading and/or mathematics, and completely homogeneous grouping. As the following chart indicates, homogeneous grouping among sampled alternative schools was virtually nonexistent.

Table 3
ABILITY-GROUPING IN CONTEMPORARY ALTERNATIVE SCHOOLS

Ability Groups	Public Elementary (5)	Nonpublic Elementary (15)	Public Secondary (6)	Nonpublic Secondary (6)	Nonpublic Combined (8)
Heterogeneous	4	13	6	6	7 = 36
Limited Homogeneous	2	2	0	0	1 = 5
Homogeneous	0	0	0	0	0 = 0

A third type of grouping is based on the mode of instruction that prevails in the school. A particular school can stress one or more of the following instructional modes: 1) large-group or lecture-based instruction, 2) small-group instruction, 3) individualized instruction, and 4) independent study. Within conventional public schools can be found examples of all four modes, though typically large-group instruction predominates.

Table 4
INSTRUCTIONAL GROUPING IN CONTEMPORARY ALTERNATIVE SCHOOLS

Instructional Grouping	Public Elementary (5)	Nonpublic Elementary (15)	Public Secondary (6)	Nonpublic Secondary (6)	Nonpublic Combined (8)
Large-group	1	1	3	1	1 = 7
Small-group	5	11	5	6	7 = 34
Individualized	5	15	2	1	6 = 29
Independent	1	14	6	6	5 = 32

Clearly the trend in instructional grouping is away from large-group teaching and toward more personalized forms of instruction. This movement stems in part from the realization by educators and parents that no one mode of instruction is best for all students. New instructional arrangements being employed in conventional public schools as well as contemporary alternatives include ad hoc learning teams, individually-contracted projects between a student and a mentor, and programmed instruction involving only the learner and his workbook.

Curriculum

The curriculum of a school embodies the learnings that some individual or group intends students to learn. These intended learnings can range from simply "learning how to learn" to a lengthy list of specific skills and contents. That the formal curriculum consists of intended learnings does not imply, however, that students do not acquire unintended learning as well. While beyond the scope of this study, an investigation of the "hidden curriculum" of alternative schools would be a valuable contribution.

One significant dimension of a curriculum is its proportion of required and elective learnings. Elementary school curricula can involve no required learnings, required work in reading and mathematics, or required work in addition to these "basics." Secondary curricula can be characterized by no elective courses, some electives, or a program based entirely on electives.

Table 5
CURRICULAR FLEXIBILITY IN CONTEMPORARY ALTERNATIVE SCHOOLS*

Options	Public Elementary (5)	Nonpublic Elementary (15)	Public Secondary (6)	Nonpublic Secondary (6)	Nonpublic Combined (8)	
Elementary:						
No requirements	0	7	—	—	2 =	9
Reading and mathematics	1	6	—	—	2 =	9
Additional requirements	4	2	—	—	1 −	7
Secondary:						
No electives	—	—	0	0	0 =	0
Some electives	—	—	4	2	3 =	9
All electives	—	—	2	4	3 =	9

*Hyphens indicate that no entry was expected for a particular item. Thus, elementary schools would not be expected to offer elective courses.

The trend, especially in nonpublic alternative schools where adherence to a state syllabus or set of official guidelines is less easy to enforce, seems to be in the direction of greater student choice of intended learnings. Seattle's public Alternative Elementary School illustrates this tendency:

> Each student must spend a required period of time each day in both a reading center and mathematics center. However, within this framework the student has available a variety of strategies through which he can learn or explore key concepts in basic skills and their application. In addition each student, with the help of his parents, may choose from a wide range of mini-courses which are changed at three week intervals to provide a variety of learning experiences.[2]

The course of studies offered at the secondary level by Philadelphia's Parkway Program is somewhat different:

> The Parkway curriculum can be broken into five basic areas, each described briefly below. These five areas can be further divided as follows: Faculty Offerings and Institutional Offerings are concerned primarily with the instruction of the student; Tutorial, Town Meeting, and Management Groups involve the student in the operation of the Program itself in an educational way. While each student puts together his own program from activities available, choosing his own ways of learning, each student will in some way be involved with all of the following activities . . . .[3]

Some nonpublic alternative schools such as Baltimore's Experimental High School and the Palfrey Street School in Watertown, Massachusetts, offer a wide range of learning experiences on a totally elective basis. These two particular schools provide a month-long winter period in which students can undertake individual projects, field trips, and intensive tutorials. Students are expected to play a predominant role in mapping out their own academic development.

In addition to curricular flexibility, a school's program of learning can be viewed in terms of the diversity of available learning opportunities. Some schools offer courses or class activities comparable to those found in a conventional public school. Others offer much fewer learning opportunities, either for reasons of philosophy or economy. Still other schools provide not only the courses found in a conventional public school, but additional courses of a more specialized, avant garde, or esoteric nature.

Table 6
DIVERSITY OF CURRICULAR OFFERINGS IN CONTEMPORARY ALTERNATIVE SCHOOLS

Options	Public Elementary (5)	Nonpublic Elementary (15)	Public Secondary (6)	Nonpublic Secondary (6)	Nonpublic Combined (8)
Equivalent to conventional public school	1	1	0	0	1 = 3
Less variety	1	10	0	4	4 = 19
More variety	3	4	6	2	3 = 18

Because of limitations of size and resources, if not imagination, nonpublic alternative schools generally are unable to provide many of the standard courses or learning opportunities available in conventional public schools. Laboratory learning and foreign language instruction are particularly lacking. Instead of these offerings, many of the smaller alternatives present a panoply of offbeat and often interdisciplinary courses ranging from Zen philosophy to hitchhiking to ecological awareness. Some schools such as Berkeley's John Muir Child Development Center shape all learning activities around a common theme, in this case the redwood tree. Other schools, notably schools-without-walls like the public C.I.T.Y. (Community Interaction Through Youth) program in Cambridge, Massachusetts, derive a variety of learning opportunities from community resource people, i.e., people in business, crafts, health professions, police work, and other occupations. As a publicity pamphlet states, "C.I.T.Y.'s course catalogue is limited only by the available resources of the Metropolitan Boston and Cambridge Communities, and it is not likely that those resources will be easily exhausted."

It is safe to conclude that the curricula of most contemporary alternative schools stress information and skills relevant to youth today. Standard methods of organizing subject matter and conventional course sequences generally are eschewed.

Instructional Features

The category "Instructional Features" is a rubric under which are grouped various aspects of teaching and learning. The following list represents a smorgasbord of instructional features that are found in some contemporary alternative schools:

1. In-and-outness (IO)—the frequent utilization of extra-classroom environments.
2. School-without-walls (SWW)—a high school in which students spend considerable time using community-based resources.
3. School-within-a-school (SWS)—a small, discrete experimental program located within a large high school.
4. Learning centers (LC)—special rooms in which students can work independently or with tutorial supervision on learning activities in a particular field.
5. Creative room arrangement (CRA)—the elimination of typical desks-in-rows format and the development of a multi-faceted, stimulating classroom environment.

6. Work-study program (WS)—student involvement for credit in a voluntary or salaried position outside of school.

7. Simultaneous use (SU)—the provision at the elementary level of a wide range of instructional materials to enable students to work on different activities at the same time.

8. Integrated day (ID)—a relatively flexible organization of time in which elementary students are permitted to work until they complete or tire of an activity rather than until the end of an arbitrary block of time.

9. Modular scheduling (MS)—a relatively flexible organization of time in which students in high school or elementary school attend classes of varying lengths.

10. Multiple staffing (Mu)—the employment of adult volunteer resource people, aides, or other personnel for supplementary instructional purposes.

11. Team teaching (TT)—the use of more than one professional teacher in the same learning situation.

12. Cross-age tutoring (CAT)—the use of older students to teach or tutor younger students.

Table 7 indicates the distribution of these instructional features through the sampled alternative schools.

The various innovative instructional features appear to be distributed somewhat unevenly across the five types of contemporary alternative school. The eleven public alternative schools account for forty-seven instructional features or slightly more than four per school. Excluding combined alternatives, the twenty-one nonpublic alternative schools account for eighty-three innovative practices or almost four per school.

A second dimension of instruction is the quality of

Table 7

INSTRUCTIONAL FEATURES OF CONTEMPORARY ALTERNATIVE SCHOOLS

Features	Public Elementary (5)	Nonpublic Elementary (15)	Public Secondary (6)	Nonpublic Secondary (6)	Nonpublic Combined (8)
IO	2	10	5	5	6 = 28
SWW	—	—	3	4	2 = 9
SWS	—	—	0	0	0 = 0
LC	2	7	3	1	1 = 14
CRA	4	8	0	0	2 = 14
WS	—	—	5	0	2 = 7
SU	5	15	—	—	3 = 23
ID	3	11	—	—	3 = 17
MS	1	2	1	0	0 = 4
Mu	5	10	4	5	7 = 31
TT	1	2	1	0	1 = 5
CAT	1	3	1	0	3 = 8

teacher-student relations. Although generalizing about types of interpersonal relations is risky, it is possible to distinguish between three basic types.

1. Professional relations in which teachers relate to students in a formalized, universalistic, superordinate way.
2. Parental relations in which teachers relate to students in an informal, though still superordinate, way.
3. Democratic relations in which teachers relate to students in an informal, particularistic, egalitarian way.

The following chart indicates the frequency of each type of teacher-student relationship among the schools in the sample.

As might be expected, professional relations tend to be found more in public alternatives than nonpublic alternatives. Democratic relations are more prevalent in non-

Table 8
TEACHER-STUDENT RELATIONS IN CONTEMPORARY ALTERNATIVE SCHOOLS

Relationship	Public Elementary (5)	Nonpublic Elementary (15)	Public Secondary (6)	Nonpublic Secondary (6)	Nonpublic Combined (8)
Professional	2	2	2	0	1 = 7
Parental	3	5	2	0	4 = 14
Democratic	0	8	2	6	3 = 19

public alternative schools. These data suggest that the teachers involved in public alternative schools may operate under different constraints or possess attitudes different from those of their colleagues in nonpublic alternatives.

Evaluation Procedures

A final dimension of schooling is evaluation—the procedure by which the nature and extent of learning is assessed. All evaluation efforts are based on certain criteria. Conventional public schools emphasize standardized testing, epitomized by nationally-normed tests, such as the Iowa Tests of Basic Skills, and classroom testing based on teacher expectations or curves. Other possible means of assessment exist. Tests can be based on individualized goals (in other words, the student competes against his past performance or potential). Criterion-referenced

Table 9
EVALUATION IN CONTEMPORARY ALTERNATIVE SCHOOLS

Basis for Evaluation	Public Elementary (5)	Nonpublic Elementary (15)	Public Secondary (6)	Nonpublic Secondary (6)	Nonpublic Combined (8)
Standardized	5	0	2	0	0 = 7
Fixed scales	0	0	3	2	1 = 6
Individualized	5	8	5	1	5 = 24
Criterion-referenced	0	2	1	0	0 = 3
No consistent evaluation	0	6	0	4	2 = 12

tests are based on a determination of whether or not a student masters a specific skill or task.

The data are somewhat surprising, in that twelve out of twenty-nine nonpublic alternative schools evidence no systematic evaluation of student progress. The remaining schools are characterized by one or more types of evaluation, though it is clear that many alternative schools prefer more individualized and less competitive assessment. This preference is indicated in a brochure describing the Community School of Philadelphia:

> At the end of each quarter, students receive a written evaluation from each of their instructors. The evaluations are designed to help students determine their strengths, weaknesses and personal progress. Students are not rated or compared with their peers; rather they are judged critically against themselves—given their aptitudes, interests and previous performance.

Variations can exist in the means employed by schools to record and report student progress. Schools can select from one or more of the following methods: conventional report cards containing alphabetical or numerical grades, written observations and student portfolios containing examples of their work, parent-teacher conferences, student-teacher conferences, and parent-student-teacher conferences. Schools also may opt not to record or report student progress.

Generally, the conference methods of reporting progress are the most popular, though the conferees differ depending on the age of the students involved. A few of the public alternatives retain the conventional system of report cards. The fact that more colleges and employers are accepting new forms of reporting student achievements, though, has encouraged the trend away from report cards and standardized testing. Whether this trend can survive the mounting pressure to assess basic skills and determine teacher accountability remains to be seen.

Table 10
REPORTING PROGRESS IN CONTEMPORARY ALTERNATIVE SCHOOLS

Method	Public Elementary (5)	Nonpublic Elementary (15)	Public Secondary (6)	Nonpublic Secondary (6)	Nonpublic Combined (8)
Report cards	3	0	1	1	1 = 6
Portfolios	0	0	4	1	2 = 7
Parent-teacher conferences	5	12	0	0	6 = 23
Student-teacher conferences	0	0	3	0	1 = 4
Parent-teacher-student conferences	0	2	0	1	0 = 3
No method of reporting	0	1	0	3	1 = 5

Historical Antecedents

Few of the innovative methods or new curricular offerings found among contemporary alternative schools are really new. Many of them first appeared during the era of progressive education that spanned the two world wars. In his masterful review of progressive education, Lawrence Cremin lists ten accomplishments of the movement:

1. Kindergartens and increased high school enrollments.
2. A six-year elementary school followed by a three-year junior high and a three-year senior high school.
3. Expansion and reorganization of the curriculum, including the addition of more practical classes.
4. Expansion of extracurricular classes.
5. More variation and flexibility in grouping students.
6. Changes in instructional methods, including an increase in student projects and a decrease in recitation.

7. Livelier and more contemporary instructional materials.
8. Architectural changes in school design.
9. Better teacher training procedures.
10. Increased bureaucratization and administrative specialization in school management.[4]

It is instructive to note that only one of the ten contributions of progressive education was concerned with the administrative organization of schools. Clearly, progressive education concentrated almost exclusively on reforms in the pedagogical characteristics of schooling.

The recent reactions against didactic and large-group instruction, homogeneous grouping, and grouping on the basis of chronological age all have antecedents among the Dalton and Winnetka Plans and one-room schoolhouses of educational history. Current changes in curriculum content and organization are echoes of past movements aimed at "hands on" or "object" learning, citizenship training, outdoor education, life adjustment courses, and the structure of the disciplines. The so-called "new" instructional features and evaluation procedures found in many contemporary alternative schools resemble earlier programs such as William Wirt's Gary Plan, with its emphasis on utilizing the resources of the city and learning by "doing."

While the historical precedents cited above tended to be found in public schools, nonpublic schools also served as occasional greenhouses for the cultivation of instructional and curricular innovations. Country day schools developed in the thirties "to spare the child the perils of the city environment in the form of doubtful companions, questionable amusements, destructive use of leisure and hazards of city streets."[5] Nonpublic schools based on the pedagogical ideas of Maria Montessori and Rudolf Steiner stressed music, singing, crafts, rhythmics, nature study, and psychomotor development. Ethical culture schools, deriving from Felix Adler's Society for Ethical Culture, provided an education based on experiential learning and values awareness.

Conclusion

So many of the instructional methods and other "technical" dimensions of contemporary alternative schools and conventional public schools are found in earlier educational experiments that one observer of recent changes contends, "classroom procedures may be similar or identical in all ways with other schools."[6] While such a statement may be exaggerated, it is apparent that contemporary alternative schools do not constitute pedagogical revolution nor do they represent reversal of educational goals. At best, it can be maintained that a handful of contemporary alternatives embody a greater concentration of progressive techniques than might be found in most earlier educational experiments. Innovation, especially in conventional public schools, has tended to be piecemeal and poorly coordinated.

The pedagogical dimensions of contemporary alternative schools do not vary drastically from one contemporary alternative to the next. Except for a few items, most public and nonpublic alternatives are remarkably alike. Only elementary and secondary alternatives display great differences, and this fact is certainly attributable, in part, to long-recognized learning variations among children and adolescents.

The conclusion is that little about the origins of contemporary alternative schools can be gleaned from an examination of their instructional features alone.

4

Contemporary Alternative Schools: Their Administrative Organization

Decisions, who make them, and how they are made, are the province of the administrative organization. In discussing the growth of the conventional public school, Michael Katz writes:

> The structure of American urban education has not changed since late in the nineteenth century; by 1880, the basic features of public education in most major cities were the same as they are today....Consider, for instance, the kindergarten, the junior high school, industrial education, testing, and the new math. Each has brought about change; but—and this is the important point—it is change *within* a given structure that itself has not altered. That is the basis on which we can claim continuity in American education over almost a century.[1]

Contemporary alternative schools may deviate from

conventional public schools in terms of specific educational goals and pedagogical features. As was seen in the last two chapters, however, the goals and pedagogical features of contemporary alternatives are not without precedent. The administrative organization of alternative schools may be a different matter, though. At least one observer argues that the structure of these recently established schools is their most "critical" characteristic:

> The revolt is no longer against outdated curricula or ineffective teaching methods—the concerns of the late 1950s and early 1960s. The revolt today is against the institution itself, against the implicit assumption that learning must be imposed on children by adults, that learning is not something one does by and for oneself, but something designated by a teacher.[2]

To some degree this analysis is overstated. Contemporary alternative schools represent not only a challenge to the structure of schooling, but to many of the goals and methods that have characterized the institution of American public schooling. The writer is correct, though, in implying that recent educational change is not simply directed at the typical problems of schools, i.e., matters of curriculum content, instructional techniques, test scores, and broad educational priorities.

The Administrative Organization of Conventional Public Schools

Though no two public schools are identical in all respects, there is justification for speaking of a conventional public school "model." Nowhere is public education more "conventional" or standardized than in the area of administrative organization.

The typical public school is organized along bureaucratic lines. Once, some small public schools were operated less bureaucratically, but over the last century the trend in public education has been toward consolidation of schools and centralization of authority. In 1930 there were approximately one hundred fifty thousand one-room schools. Three decades later there were about fifteen thousand. The number of school districts dwindled from one hundred thirty thousand to twenty thousand.[3]

Consolidation and centralization are two traits of the process of bureaucratization. Most bureaucracies can be characterized by the six basic qualities first outlined by Max Weber:

1. Division of labor and specialization of tasks
2. Hierarchical authority structure
3. Formal system of rules and regulations governing official decisions
4. Separate administrative and productive staffs
5. Impersonal, universalistic orientation to clients
6. Career employment for bureaucratic officials[4]

That public schools conform to these traits is attested to by most researchers. In a typical reference, Ronald Corwin's *A Sociology of Education,* the author writes,

> Authority tends to be organized along hierarchical lines in public schools. In large systems there are several levels of authority, perhaps including a department head, assistant principals, systemwide supervisors and other assistants to the superintendent, school board members, lay advisory committees, and county and state supervisory agencies. Officials at each level face the dual problem of satisfying their subordinates and their superiors.[5]

Corwin goes on to observe that the school's authority structure sometimes can differ from its power structure. He cites the instances of a secretary who handles scheduling of classes and a custodian who determines how space is assigned.

In the conventional public school, the teacher's role is that of a "functionary." Sloan Wayland argues that the teacher is a "replaceable unit in a rationally organized system, and most of the significant aspects of work are determined for him."[6] Rising teacher militancy and union activity are resulting in more power for teachers as a group, yet individual teachers still function largely at the discretion of the school administration.

Citizens are not any better off than teachers. The power they exercise is largely negative. They can reject board members, bonds, and budgets, but rarely can they exert a positive or innovative influence over the school system. Parent-teacher organizations and citizens' advisory groups seem to exist more for the efficient dissemination of information from above than the generation of pressure for educational improvement from below.

Types of Administrative Organization in Contemporary Alternatives

Researching contemporary alternative schools revealed a number of relatively distinct patterns of administrative organization. Based on the people involved in making decisions, a typology with nine variations was created and used to classify schools in the sample.

Parent Cooperative type (PC). Teachers and parents share decision-making authority. They enjoy one vote apiece. Many decisions are made in large-group meetings on a consensus basis. This type of administrative organization is designed to stimulate a feeling of community reminiscent of the traditional New England town meetings. In many cases, parent cooperatives can be seen as "surrogate communes."[7]

Parent-Teacher type (PT). This type differs from the previous one in that there is a distinct division of responsibilities between parents and teachers. Parents typically meet as a group or in committees to handle matters pertaining to hiring, finances, and facilities. Teachers deal with day-to-day decisions, including ones concerned with discipline, evaluation and academic program.

Parent-Teacher-Administrator type (PTA). This type of administrative organization is identical to the previous one except that decision-making power is shared with an elected or appointed administrator. The administrator may be a parent volunteer, a teacher, or a person hired especially for the position. The administrator functions more as a coordinator than as a leader.

Teacher-Administrator type (TA). A division of responsibilities exists between the teaching staff and an elected or appointed administrator. This type resembles the conventional public school model, but for the fact that teachers generally exercise more decision-making power in the alternative school setting.

Headmaster type (H). Most decision-making power is vested in the hands of the headmaster or principal. Traditional alternative schools often are characterized by the headmaster type of administrative organization. Typically, the headmaster is accountable only to a Board of Trustees.

Teacher type (T). Teachers exercise virtually complete control over decision-making processes. Often, the teachers themselves have children in the school.

Student type (S). Though they rely on adults as resource persons, students make most of the decisions pertaining to school policy, programs, and evaluation. This type of administrative organization is found exclusively at the secondary level.

Student-Teacher Cooperative type (STC). Similar to the parent cooperative format, this type involves minimal division of responsibility between teachers and students. They share decision-making power with every person exercising an equal vote. Again, this type of administrative organization is found only at the secondary level.

Student-Teacher-Administrator type (STA). A division

of responsibilities exists between the three parties. Students make decisions with teachers concerning day-to-day operations. Teachers determine the academic program and the bases for evaluation. The elected or appointed administrator coordinates school affairs, handles finances, and sets broad policy.

In addition to these nine types of administrative organization, contemporary alternative schools also may be characterized by no stable decision-making patterns.

Data on Types of Administrative Organization

The following table records the results of an analysis of the administrative organization of the sampled schools. The schools are classified according to their *original* organizational format. Obviously, many of the forty schools underwent changes in personnel and organization. These changes tended to be in the direction of more divisional responsibility and generally decreasing parental involvement. The influence of teachers on decision-making processes increased over time.

Table 11

ADMINISTRATIVE ORGANIZATION IN CONTEMPORARY ALTERNATIVE
SCHOOLS

Type	Public Elementary (5)	Nonpublic Elementary (15)	Public Secondary (6)	Nonpublic Secondary (6)	Nonpublic Combined (8)	
PC	0	7	0	0	2 =	9
PT	0	2	0	0	3 =	5
PTA	1	3	0	0	0 =	4
TA	4	0	1	1	0 =	6
H	0	0	1	0	0 =	1
T	0	2	1	0	1 =	4
S	0	0	0	1	0 =	1
STC	0	0	0	3	2 =	5
STA	0	0	3	1	0 =	4
No stable administrative organization	0	1	0	0	0 =	1

No type of administrative organization predominates in all contemporary alternatives. Public alternatives are not represented in certain categories, notably parent and student-teacher cooperatives. Parental involvement, in fact, does not characterize public alternatives in general. Parents are also absent from decision-making processes in most secondary schools, in part because students are old enough to assume responsibility themselves.

Predictably, very few contemporary alternative schools opted for a conventional type of administrative organization. Six schools, including four out of five public elementary schools, chose a relatively conventional teacher-administrator type of administrative organization. Even in these instances, however, the teachers tended to exercise more power than in most conventional public schools. One school manifested the headmaster type of administrative organization. Otherwise, the remaining thirty-three alternative schools represented efforts to involve groups of people typically left out of the mainstream of educational decision-making—parents, students, and to a lesser extent, teachers. The next question concerns the ways decisions are made by these groups. Do these decision-making processes also reflect a rejection of the conventional bureaucratic format of most public schools?

Data on Decision-Making Processes

The previous discussion pinpointed the different arrangements of people involved in operating contemporary alternative schools. Nothing was said about the decision-making procedures they utilize. A variety of processes and special roles can characterize educational decision-making. Those that were anticipated to exist in contemporary alternative schools are listed below:

1. meeting of the school community at large
2. elected or appointed committees
3. faculty meeting
4. advisory groups (i.e., P-TA groups)

5. elected Board of Trustees
6. appointed Board of Trustees
7. elected or appointed Coordinator
8. Headmaster (broad discretionary powers)
9. autonomous teachers
10. cluster or team planning among teachers
11. consultant advisory service

These decision-making processes and provisions do not represent all possibilities, only the ones occurring in the greatest frequencies in the pilot studies and the existing literature concerning alternative schools. The following table is based on the actual decision-making processes that characterized the sampled schools at the time of their establishment. It should be noted that virtually every school in the sample underwent changes in these processes during its first year or two of operation. More than one decision-making process can characterize a particular school in the sample. Thus, it is possible for a given contemporary alternative school to reach decisions by meetings of the school community, faculty meetings, and the actions of an appointed coordinator.

Knowing the legal constraints on the organization of public schools, it is not surprising that public alternatives do not evidence exactly the same distribution of decision-making arrangements as nonpublic alternatives. Public alternative schools are more directly accountable to a central or district administration, which includes a superintendent or chief school officer and an elected board of education.

Nonpublic schools also exist under the aegis of a local educational authority, but they tend to enjoy more organizational latitude. State departments of education often have no rigid guidelines governing the structure of nonpublic alternatives, particularly elementary schools. The only administrative requirement for incorporation as a school typically is the selection of a board of trustees. Many alternative schools appoint a board of trustees on "paper," while actually relying on other decision-making procedures.

In contrast to contemporary alternatives, the decision-

Table 12
DECISION-MAKING PROCESSES IN CONTEMPORARY ALTERNATIVE SCHOOLS

D-M Process	Public Elementary (5)	Nonpublic Elementary (15)	Public Secondary (6)	Nonpublic Secondary (6)	Nonpublic Combined (8)
School Meeting	1	13	3	6	5 = 28
Committees	2	2	0	1	3 = 8
Faculty Meetings	4	7	5	3	5 = 24
Advisory Groups	2	0	0	0	0 = 2
Board of Trustees (elected)	—	3	—	2	2 = 7
Board of Trustees (appointed)	—	2	—	0	2 = 4
Coordinator	2	3	4	4	4 = 17
Headmaster or Director	3	2	2	0	0 = 7
Autonomous Teachers	3	0	2	0	0 = 5
Teacher Teams	2	1	1	0	0 = 4
Consultants	2	0	1	0	0 = 3

making processes found in most traditional alternative schools lack democratic qualities:

> The governance of most private schools is on paper relatively simple. The typical independent school operates on the basis of a charter which provides for a self-perpetuating board of trustees. In principle all powers and policy decisions are the board's, though in practice it delegates full administrative authority as well as certain policymaking powers to the school head, to be exercised by him at his discretion but with the advice and consent of the board. The head is thus the pivot of the organization as well as the primary channel of communication between the school and its various constituencies.[8]

Otto Kraushaar describes faculty influence as primarily informal, based on "working agreements" with the head. As for parental or student involvement in decision making, Kraushaar finds that, in traditional alternative schools, "parents and students usually have little or no power in the sense of a right to vote on matters of substance affecting the school."[9]

Having noted the characteristics of conventional public schools and traditional nonpublic schools, it is necessary to shift attention back to the numerous ways in which contemporary alternative schools, (both public and nonpublic), are organized. Contemporary alternatives generally minimize or reject entirely many of the trappings of bureaucracies: centralization of authority, specialization of function, and standardization of procedures. Earlier, it was seen that parents, students, and teachers have been brought more directly into school governance in many contemporary alternatives. This movement to increase participation in decision-making is accomplished through the "town meeting" in many nonpublic alternative schools. Frequently lasting hours, these meetings provide an opportunity for all members of the school community to air grievances, socialize, express opinions, and suggest improvements. Decisions often are reached by consensus, though this process is an arduous one for many groups.

In public alternatives, on the other hand, increased participation in decision-making is achieved largely through a reduction in the power of administrators and an increase in the opportunities for faculty members and, occasionally, students to influence school policies. Working as a faculty, on committees, in clusters or teams, and as semi-autonomous professionals, teachers in public alternative schools generally enjoy much more decision-making responsibility than their colleagues in conventional public schools and traditional alternative schools.

Students also enjoy increased involvement in decision-making, both in public and nonpublic alternatives. Instead of electing members of "rubber stamp" student councils, students in the secondary alternative schools which have been

created during the last decade have found themselves operating town meetings and committees, voting on the hiring
of teachers and courses to be offered, and contributing to
the development of school rules and regulations.

Though seven schools in the sample employed administrators reminiscent of the traditional headmaster, seven-
teen public and nonpublic alternatives opted for a coordinator instead. Five of these coordinators were elected, while
the others were appointed. The role of coordinator differs
from that of headmaster, director, or principal in that it
involves more maintenance functions and fewer leadership
functions. Coordinators see that meetings are scheduled,
tuitions are collected, newsletters are mailed, and materials
are purchased.

The data concerning who makes decisions and how
those decisions are made clearly indicate that contemporary
alternative schools are not simply reactions against pedagogical aspects of conventional schooling. Contemporary alternatives constitute a direct challenge to the way schools
have been organized and administered.

Historical Antecedents

Educational history reveals that many, if not most, of
the goals and pedagogical methods characterizing contemporary alternative schools have been incorporated in earlier
efforts to transform the schools. Do recent attempts to alter
the decision-making structure of schools have similar
precedents?

Lately, the decision-making structure of schools has
received considerable attention by historians and sociologists. They have found clues to social development in the
ways institutions change. Most of the writing concerns public education, though Otto Kraushaar provides an analysis
of organizational change in nonpublic schools:

> By way of summary, one can see a gradual but
> significant shift toward an increase in sharing

power or influence among various constituencies of the nonpublic school. In the nineteenth century, the governing boards of schools normally containing a generous complement of clergymen, commonly shared the decision-making powers in important matters with school heads, who were frequently invested with dictatorial authority. Since then, the growth of academic professionalism has greatly increased the faculty's influence in decision-making, so that the prevailing pattern finds the school head, no longer the benevolent autocrat of old, sharing his powers with the faculty, while the trustees' role is (except among the Protestant schools) restricted to choosing a new head, watching over the institution's financial welfare and real estate, and advising on matters which the school head brings to their attention. In the process of gradual democratization the teachers and, to a still limited extent, the students have acquired a stronger voice, usually at the expense of the authority formerly exercised by the head and the trustees. Parental influence is generally somewhat stronger in the church schools than among the independents, and in the parent-owned Protestant schools there is considerable parent-involvement in school affairs.[10]

Kraushaar detects the gradual evolution of nonpublic school organization in the direction of more participatory decision-making. He offers little evidence, however, to indicate that such a movement was actually afoot before the mid-sixties. With a few exceptions at the time of the utopian experiments of the previous century and during the more recent era of progressive education, nonpublic alternatives have not experienced the fundamental organizational changes that contemporary alternatives have undergone. Most of the experimental alternative schools of previous years limited their innovations to new approaches to childrearing, instructional techniques, and curricula.

In regard to public education, the works of Michael Katz, Joseph Cronin, Richard Pratte, and Joel Spring strongly imply that the administrative organization of public schools likewise has not changed markedly in almost a century.

The growth of the public school in nineteenth century America was an event long memorialized by educational historians such as Ellwood P. Cubberley as the triumph of a free society and the very embodiment of democracy.[11] Revisionist historians are less enthusiastic. They suspiciously note that the public school adopted a bureaucratic form of organization at the same time that the nation was undergoing an industrial revolution. Sheer coincidence is not advanced as an explanation.

Arnold Foster contends that the fantastic growth in production during the last half of the nineteenth century was due as much to the American genius for bureaucratic organization as to sheer Yankee inventiveness.[12] Were students subject to the same "laws" that applied to manufacturing? Was it only natural that an organizational model which worked so well for developing industries would be adopted by public schools?

Pratte and Katz point out that the bureaucratic model was not the only alternative available in the late eighteen hundreds. Pratte states:

> Public schools might have become supplementary agencies, like libraries, attached to small neighborhood community. Schools might have become coordinating agencies, serving to guide and direct students into a variety of educational experiences provided by the economic, cultural, political, etc. institutions.[13]

Katz indicates that the bureaucratic model was simply one of four available organizational forms, the others being paternalistic voluntarism, democratic localism, and corporate voluntarism.

A combination of *noblesse oblige* and benevolent autocracy, paternalistic voluntarism can be interpreted to be the precursor of compensatory alternative education.[14] Students from poor families and orphans went to these schools in order to be "salvaged" from lives of utter despair and trained for the semiskilled jobs that constituted the backbone of American industrial ascendance.

The first option to paternalistic voluntarism was democratic localism, born out of the era of Jacksonian democracy.[15] Katz paraphrases theorist Orestes Brownson's description of this organizational model when he notes that "each vital interest remained within the smallest possible unit, of which the very smallest would be the (school) district."[16] Democratic localism, for all its encouragement of citizen participation and cooperation, was a relatively inefficient form of administrative organization. It became more practical to seek alternatives as the United States grew and school districts burgeoned. Katz concludes:

> For, in the last analysis, the rejection of democratic localism rested only partly on its inefficiency and violation of parental prerogative. It stemmed equally from a gut fear of the cultural divisiveness inherent in the increasing religious and ethnic diversity of American life. Cultural homogenization played counterpoint to administrative rationality. Bureaucracy was intended to standardize far more than the conduct of public life.[17]

This process of cultural homogenization is discussed at length in Cronin's book, *The Control of Urban Schools.*

If paternalistic voluntarism and democratic localism were too unsophisticated or inappropriate for a growing industrial nation, incipient bureaucracy still had to contend with corporate voluntarism. This organizational model, when applied to schools, was based on a self-perpetuating board of trustees. Finances were derived from endowments and tuition payments.[18] Corporate voluntarism characterized most secondary schools and colleges up until the late nineteenth century. It continues to linger in the form of voucher schemes, tax credit systems, and other "free enterprises" solutions to current educational problems.

Eventually, the bureaucratic organizational model prevailed, despite the existence of alternatives. Why was this model selected? Was the choice an accident, the only logical choice, or the product of a dark capitalist conspiracy? Pratte correctly observes that a shift as sweeping as that "from an unsystematic pattern of schools to a full-scale bureaucratization of schools represents a major ideological commitment."[19] Katz reiterates this observation:

> Bureaucracy is not a neutral form; it represents the crystallization of particular social values. In America those values have expressed, and worked for, class interests.[20]

While none of the revisionist historians suggests that the commitment to bureaucracy was the product of a carefully planned conspiracy of industrial and business interests, each notes that the people who were in a position to make educational decisions in the late nineteenth and early twentieth centuries represented upper middle-class economic interests.

Horace Mann and Henry Barnard, among others, championed bureaucratic organization, seeing in it the virtues of efficiency, economy, and freedom from ward politics. It is this last aspect of American urban education that has received the most attention recently. As large metropolitan areas absorbed more and more immigrants, they came under the control of ethnically-based ward bosses. School boards reflected neighborhood power patterns. Labeled as corrupt and inefficient, these boards of education, as well as ward politics in general, became the subjects of a major crusade in the late nineteenth century. Reformers from various upper middle-class backgrounds—businessmen, professors, and civic leaders—sought to centralize urban education, thereby reducing the number of neighborhood school boards and wresting control from working class interests. Cronin concludes that,

> ... the move from ward-based school boards to central boards also shifted power from the working class to the upper class and to more cosmopolitan professionals who claimed to be revolted by disclosures of inefficiency and corruption. Henceforth, the schools would be run by a "guardian" class who because of their own superior education presumably knew what kind of schools should be maintained.[21]

That public education is still in the hands of special interest groups is the contention of Joel Spring. He does not see the bureaucratic form of organization as the culprit. Rather, he argues that the subtleties of "the process of schooling," a somewhat ill-defined construct, are to blame for the failure of public schools to develop alternatives for students from various socioeconomic backgrounds. He states,

> The significance of the American high school was not the content of its curriculum but the social process of clubs, student government, differentiation, and all the extra-curricular activities which socialized the individual for the benefit of the corporate state.[22]

What Spring and a number of other observers of American institutions seem to ignore is the intimate relationship between organizational goals, processes, and structure. For example, bureaucratic structure presumably designed to provide for the efficient coordination of services, winds up exerting a pervasive influence over the very nature of the services themselves.

The Influence of Structure on Function

The development of most organizations is considered to involve a relatively constant series of steps: selection of goals, selection of an administrative structure to facilitate the achievement of the goals, selection of personnel to staff the organization, and actual operation of the organization. A rationally conceived organization implies a decision-making model which best serves the goals of the organization. The assumption is that the goals dictate the appropriate form of administrative organization, not the reverse. This assumption, however, is not always valid. Structure can dictate function. The goal of student literacy, for instance, can be influenced by a bureaucratic organization in ways different from a democratic or a paternalistic organization. Bureaucracies especially are noted for the phenomenon of "goal displacement," whereby the original goals or functions of the organization are subordinated to the internal goals of perpetuating the existing organization and maintaining stability.

The close relationship between structure and function in educational organizations has been recognized by a few astute observers in the past. For example, radical Spanish educator Francisco Ferrer, who was hanged in 1910 for treason, wrote that "the organization of the school, far from spreading the ideal which we imagined, has made education the most powerful means of enslavement in the hands of governing powers today."[23] Bureaucratization means centralization, and, where centralization occurs, the tendency is for individual participation in decision-making to be reduced.

A. S. Neill also understood how the processes by which educational decisions are made influence *which* decisions are made. Aside from Ferrer, Neill, and a few muckrackers like Upton Sinclair, the majority of those who have scrutinized the educational process in this century seem more concerned with teaching techniques, testing, and curriculum content than with the administrative organizations of schools.

John Dewey, that most erudite of educational theorists, virtually ignored the structure of schools. In his *Democracy and Education* he mentions school administration only three times.[24] Never does he discuss the processes by which educational decisions are made. Instead he concentrated on pedagogical matters. His primary contributions are summarized by Harry Broudy. Broudy contends that Dewey persuaded the most famous educators of the three decades from 1930 to 1960 that "learning academic subjects was not the primary goal of schooling" and that "the method of problem solving so successful in the sciences could be adapted to groupthinking about social problems."[25] Only one of the ten accomplishments of progressive education listed by Lawrence Cremin was concerned with administrative matters. This accomplishment encompassed the growth of school administration as a profession independent of teaching and the subsequent increased bureaucratization of public education.[26] Michael Katz concludes that progressive education failed to alter fundamentally the structure of American education:

> It failed partly because it suffered from the weaknesses of earlier reform movements. It failed as well because it did not even try. For the most part, progressivism represented a conservative movement that accepted the structure of American education as it was and tried to work changes within that framework.[27]

Progressive education manifested little regard for town meetings, parent cooperatives, or schools run by students and teachers. John Dewey issued neither a challenge to the principle of hierarchical organization nor a directive to work toward participatory democracy in the management of schools.

Through the decades of the forties and fifties, the stress in education circles continued to be placed on curriculum content, instructional methodology, and other pedagogical matters. The extent of most educators' interest in school administration was a relatively naive faith in the fact that bureaucratic organization ensured businesslike efficiency.[28]

Spring is probably correct when he characterizes criticism of schools in the past fifty years as "shallow."[29] It is too simple to presume that the constant trend toward the bureaucratization of education has not exerted a marked influence over the functions of public schools—an influence many regard as deleterious. Particularly in the past decade, critics of American education have impugned the bureaucratization of public schools and called for radical changes. The most radical proposals are those advocated by Ivan Illich and Everett Reimer. These men suggest the need for dismantling schools as institutions and establishing informal networks of educational resource centers and systems of apprenticeships. Other proposals, represented by contemporary alternative schools, call for the continuation of schools, but with the development of new, more democratic decision-making structures. One spokesman for alternative schools, Robert Riordan, captures the essence of these more moderate critiques:

> The reader will note that we devote more of our discussion to issues of *process*—who makes decisions, how people relate to each other, and how the school defines itself relative to the system—than to program content. This emphasis is consistent with the general emphasis in alternative schools, which frequently develops out of a concern with the so-called hidden curriculum: the effect of the structure and process of schooling independent of curriculum content. Therefore, their concern is not so much with designing effective learning packages, but with creating a setting where students can play an active, creative role in deciding the direction their education should take. They wish to create a school community which is itself a model for that process in its relations with other institutions.[30]

Though he uses the term "process," Riordan essentially is

speaking about the administrative organization of contemporary alternative schools as their "critical" factor.

Others are recognizing that basic changes in education cannot occur without transforming the processes by which educational decisions are made and increasing the types of people involved directly in making decisions. At the first International Convention on Options in Public Education, held in Minneapolis in the fall of 1973, a number of speakers and participants addressed themselves to the necessity of structural change in schools.[31] Don Davies, previously a top-level bureaucrat in the Office of Education and now in charge of Boston University's Institute for Responsive Education, expressed the belief that many contemporary alternatives are the reactions of well-to-do white parents to the "encrusted bureaucratic structure" of public schools and to growing teacher professionalism—two dimensions of public schooling that serve to separate those who "consume" education from those who "produce" it.

Dwight Allen, one-time dean of the innovative School of Education at the University of Massachusetts, disagreed with Davies. He argued at the convention that the problem with education is not that bureaucrats and militant professionals are in control, but that no one is in control. One of the disturbing challenges of a bureaucracy such as the public school system is to locate someone who actually is accountable to the public for his actions.

Besides Davies and Allen, others spoke about the need for organizational change. Vernon Smith, a co-director of the National Consortium on Options in Public Education, contended that people have been concerned with the functions of schools since the days of Socrates, but that the average person still has little to say about what schools accomplish. Along with Mario Fantini, Smith considered the culprit to be the "institutional arrangement" of public schools. Decision-making in schools must become more accessible to the public, lest the schools serve as a blatant contradiction to the ideals of a democratic society. Ironically, many of the people who attended the convention accused Smith and the other people who planned the affair of being inaccessible to outside influence, particularly influence from persons active in nonpublic alternative education.

Harold Hodgkinson offers one of the best statements describing the intensifying interest in the need for structural change in schools:

> We spend, in education, considerable time formu-
> lating the functions we wish the schools to per-
> form. Every college catalog, every high school bro-
> chure gives a very clear, often noble and inspiring
> view of the functions that school or college per-
> forms. What is being suggested here is that the
> educational structure may not be well adapted to
> meet these functions. There is a real dearth of
> thinking about alternative ways of structuring
> educational institutions so that they might fulfill,
> in a more genuine, effective way, the functions we
> now say (and fervently hope) they do.[32]

Hodgkinson concludes that we "need to give thought to both structure and function, realizing that new functions may well require new structures."[33]

The increasing awareness of the need for structural change is being expressed in professional circles by social scientists and innovative educators. Community pressures for greater control over local schools, demands for account-ability by professionals, and exploration of voucher schemes are manifestations of a similar awareness on the part of laymen.[34] People want more responsive, less impersonal schools, not to mention other public service organizations. Many people also feel that the bureaucratic form or organi-zation is unnecessarily costly, due in part to the large num-ber of supervisory personnel.

Unlike the varied goals and pedagogical dimensions of contemporary alternative schools, their variety of struc-tural options—from town meetings to coordinators to committees of students, parents, and teachers—lack significant precedents in American educational history. Little attention has been paid previously to increasing the participation of students, parents, and individual teachers in educational decision-making. Why contemporary alternative schools suddenly should have undertaken to increase participation and, in so doing, transform the administrative organization of schools is the focus of the remaining chapters. Allen Graubard sums up the situation in the following way:

> Until we get clear on why centralization took place ... we will be misconceiving the significance of radical school reform and its potential. To ascribe some abstract "lust for control" to all bureaucracies can obscure the analysis of who gets controlled and who does the controlling of the bureaucracy and for what purposes and in whose interests.[35]

Even more specifically to the point, Marilyn Cohn and Mary Ellen Finch conclude that,

> ...the source of the alternative school idea and the way it has been operationalized was an attempt to meet the individual's need for personal integrity and fulfillment within a highly organized technical society or, as it translates into the school context, the needs of individuals within a large, impersonal school organization.[36]

5

Contemporary Alternative Schools: Their Composition

The goals, methods, and administrative organization of contemporary alternative schools having been described, it remains to determine the types of people involved in their operation. Earlier, it was noted that recent alternatives seem to cater to competent students from middle-class backgrounds. Are these schools, in fact, populated primarily by such students? Do parents and teachers who support and staff alternative schools possess any common characteristics that could assist in advancing explanations for the emergence of the schools?

Students

Gathering data on students in contemporary alternatives was a difficult matter, since detailed records on students rarely existed and, where they did, lacked consistency. The hypothesized make-up of contemporary alternatives presented in Chapter 1 included two basic student characteristics. First, students were anticipated to be generally capable of succeeding in conventional public schools. In other words, they were not considered to be subject to serious learning deficiencies, physical handicaps, or major disciplinary problems. Second, students were expected to come mostly from white, middle- and upper-middle-class families.

No means of assessing the level of student ability was available to the author other than a set of impressionistic observations. Teachers, students, and sometimes parents were asked whether the youngsters enrolled in the school generally had successful or unsuccessful public school experiences immediately prior to entering the alternative school. Unsuccessful public school experience was based on the existence of recorded disciplinary, emotional, or serious motivational problems. A capable student who was withdrawn from a conventional public school because he did not have enough opportunity for artistic activity or because he had personality clashes with a particular teacher would not be characterized as a student having had an unsuccessful experience.

The people who were interviewed were asked whether more than approximately one-quarter of the students definitely could be described as unsuccessful public school students. They were asked whether a similar percentage of students had enjoyed previously successful public school experiences.

In certain instances involving elementary alternative schools, a large number of students had no public school experience at all. Often, however, the students had been involved in preschools and day-care centers.

Where large numbers of students came from different educational backgrounds, two entries were made for an alternative school in the sample. Thus, the chart below might contain a school that enrolled substantial percentages of students with both successful and unsuccessful public school experiences.

Table 13

THE EDUCATIONAL BACKGROUND OF STUDENTS IN CONTEMPORARY
ALTERNATIVE SCHOOLS

Previous Educational Experience	Public Elementary (5)	Nonpublic Elementary (15)	Public Secondary (6)	Nonpublic Secondary (6)	Nonpublic Combined (8)
Successful in Public School	5	7	6	6	5 = 29
Unsuccessful in Public School	0	5	3	6	5 = 19
Nonpublic School Only	0	2	0	1	1 = 4
Day-Care or Preschool	1	6	—	—	2 = 9

The data indicate that nineteen out of forty alternative schools enrolled at least one quarter of their students with unsuccessful public school experiences. Fifteen of these nineteen also enrolled significant numbers of students with successful public school experiences immediately prior to transfer. Only four alternatives enrolled large numbers of students with only nonpublic school backgrounds. All of these were themselves nonpublic schools.

While the generalization holds that contemporary alternative schools attract competent students, it is also obvious that other kinds of students are represented. If the experience of Philadelphia's Parkway Program—one of the first public alternative schools, having opened in 1969— is indicative, contemporary alternative schools can attract a diverse student body. In a description of the formal evaluation of Parkway that was completed by the Organization for Social and Technical Innovation (OSTI), Leonard Finkelstein writes,

> OSTI's definition of the student population best served by Parkway met with some opposition from Parkway parents, students, and staff. While it was agreed that Parkway does serve the three groups mentioned in the report 1) some of the

most academically talented students who find themselves turned off by regular schooling; 2) the nonconforming, rebellious students; and 3) low-skilled, low income minority students, it was felt that Parkway is also serving a group which was omitted: the average student who is doing well in a traditional school setting, but who is also somewhat of a risk-taker, and is therefore willing or anxious to try something new. This is an important group of students at Parkway which may have been overlooked. [Italics omitted.][1]

The only generalization that really applies to students in contemporary alternative schools is that no generalization fits them all.

Parents

In most instances students do not enroll in an alternative school without first securing parental permission. As was indicated in the previous chapter, parents often become involved more extensively than simply granting permission. Especially in nonpublic elementary and combined elementary-secondary alternatives, they help make decisions, serve on committees, pay tuition, engage in fund-raising activities, act as volunteer teachers and aides, and often actually establish new schools. In twenty-two of the forty schools in the sample, a parent or group of parents was responsible for starting the school. Half of this number included parents who recently had moved into the area in which the alternative was located. This fact suggests that many parents who support contemporary alternative schools are in the process of seeking new economic and educational opportunities.

In order to determine whether any generalizations can be made about alternative school parents, a series of questions was asked during the onsite interviews. The questions were designed more to capture a general impression of the subjects than to obtain a statistically precise breakdown of "types" of parents. Where possible, though, actual counts were made to determine the proportions of parents possessing particular characteristics. The following questions were asked:

1. Do roughly half or more of the students come from families in which both parents are living together?
2. Can roughly half or more of the parents be characterized as middle class?
3. Can at least one-fourth of the parents be characterized as working class?
4. Can at least one-fourth of the parents be characterized as upper-middle or upper class?
5. Are the majority of parents white?
6. Are at least one-fourth of the parents non-white?
7. Are at least one-fourth of the mothers employed outside the home?
8. Are at least one-fourth of the parents experimenting with new lifestyles (i.e., communal living, group marriage, voluntary subsistence living, "back-to-the-land" situations, etc.)?
9. Are at least one-fourth of the parents new to the locality in which the school is located (i.e., having resided in the locality less than three years)?
10. Can a majority of parents be characterized by liberal-to-radical political beliefs?
11. Are at least one-fourth of the families represented by at least one parent employed in a service-oriented profession (law, medicine, education, psychology, etc.)?

The data on parent characteristics bear out the hypothesis that contemporary alternative schools are supported largely by a white, middle-class clientele. Further, the parents generally conform to descriptions of Americans most inclined to support new ideas. One research study describes change-minded people in the following manner:

They are generally young, have relatively high

Table 14
CHARACTERISTICS OF PARENTS IN CONTEMPORARY
ALTERNATIVE SCHOOLS

Parent Traits	Public Elementary (5)	Nonpublic Elementary (15)	Public Secondary (6)	Nonpublic Secondary (6)	Nonpublic Combined (8)
50% or more families intact	5	6	6	5	3 = 25
50% or more middle class*	5	14	5	5	8 = 37
25% or more working class*	2	2	4	1	3 = 12
25% or more upper-middle or upper class*	0	1	2	3	1 = 7
50% or more white	5	15	5	6	8 = 39
25% or more non-white	2	1	1	1	4 = 9
25% or more working mothers	1	8	0	1	2 = 12
25% or more new lifestyles	1	10	0	1	5 = 17
25% or more new residents	1	10	1	3	3 = 18
50% or more liberal beliefs	1	10	0	3	4 = 18
25% or more professional parents	1	4	2	3	3 = 13

*Middle class status is based on one or both parents having college education and being employed in a skilled position. Working class status i based on a lesser degree of education (high school or lower) and employment in a blue-collar, semi-skilled, or menial position. Upper-middle and upper class status is based on relatively higher levels of education and income than characterize middle-class parents. Often one or both parents are professionals.

social status (high prestige ratings, greater education, and greater income), are cosmopolitan in outlook, use impersonal and cosmopolitan sources of information, exert opinion leadership, and are likely to be viewed as deviants by their peers and themselves.[2]

Parent characteristics expectedly differ between elementary and secondary alternatives. The parents of secondary school students generally are older and tend to be more conservative in lifestyle. Parents are less directly involved in secondary school activities, in part because their children are mature enough to assume many decision-making responsibilities and managerial functions themselves. Parents of secondary school students are also less prone than parents of younger students to be the driving force behind the creation of alternative schools.

All generalizations, of course, invite exceptions. A few nonpublic secondary alternatives in the sample were the product of parent initiative. The description of the birth of New York City's Elizabeth Cleaners Street School is illustrative of parent-initiated high schools:

> A family I knew told me that a number of people were getting together with the intention of setting up a free-alternate-street school in Manhattan's Upper West Side. The idea for the school began when Sema Salit was walking out of a depressing meeting at a supposedly liberal private school her daughter attended. She decided that if she and her daughter couldn't find a school capable of meeting the needs of her daughter, she would create one.[3]

As a rule, however, parents of high school students are found to be less change-minded and less directly involved in school business than their counterparts in nonpublic elementary and combined elementary-secondary alternatives.

The parents of elementary-age students, particularly those involved in nonpublic alternatives, tend to deviate from "typical" parents in conventional public schools in terms of their lifestyles, habits, and attitudes. Nine of fifteen nonpublic alternatives enrolling strictly elementary-age children had a majority of students from one-parent families. In fact, several schools enrolled as many as ninety percent of their students from families which had experienced separation, divorce, or out-of-wedlock births. Typically, a one-parent family involved a child or children and a mother. Consequently, it was not surprising that eight out of fifteen nonpublic elementary alternatives boasted at least one-fourth working mothers.

The parents involved in nonpublic alternatives also tend to share a pattern of living marked by social experimentation, transience, and liberal-to-radical political beliefs. Out of fifteen nonpublic elementary alternatives, ten had significant numbers of parents sharing these three traits.

Differences are found between parents of public school and nonpublic school students. Working class representation is proportionately greater in public alternatives, though overall it is low. No public alternative school is characterized by a majority of one-parent families. Public school parents engaging in new lifestyles or manifesting avant garde habits almost never constitute as much as a quarter of the entire parent body.

It might be expected, on the basis of the preceding findings, that the factors accounting for parent support of public alternative schools are not identical to those influencing parents in nonpublic alternatives. Similarly, elementary and combined elementary-secondary alternatives seem to derive from factors somewhat different from those affecting secondary alternative schools. It is again apparent that no simple explanation can account for the phenomenon of contemporary alternative schools.

Teachers

It is most unlikely that contemporary alternative schools would have developed without an available reservoir of dissatisfied people willing to function as teachers, volunteers, tutors, facilitators, and coordinators. Many experienced teachers have tolerated drastic reductions in salaries and benefits in order to work in the more flexible environment characterizing most alternative schools. Many alternative schools rely on community "resource" people and parent or college-student volunteers to supplement the regular teaching staff and provide a more desirable teacher-student ratio. Teaching staffs range from one or two full-time teachers in the smaller nonpublic elementary alternatives to sixty or more in the larger public high school alternatives.

Do the adults who teach in contemporary alternatives possess any common characteristics that might assist in explaining the dramatic development of these schools? Sample schools were classified according to whether they employed more than one salaried teacher who had

1. taught for at least three years
2. taught from one to three years
3. no teaching experience
4. received teacher training in college
5. received a college degree without any teacher training
6. been unemployed immediately prior to working in the alternative school
7. one or more children enrolled in the alternative school
8. experimented with alternative or radical lifestyles

As with students and parents, the data reveal that teachers in contemporary alternative schools come from diverse backgrounds. Because of certification requirements, public alternative schools employ virtually no teachers who lack special training. Less expectedly, perhaps, all but one public alternative school employ teachers with three or more years of professional experience. A large number of these individuals are teachers in their late twenties, thirties, and early forties who have tried with varying degrees of success to innovate in conventional settings. They turn to public alternative schools because they can do what they have done for years without as much "red tape" and administrative interference. Teachers in public alternatives, though dissatisfied in general with the quality of American education, do not tend to manifest countercultural habits

Table 15
TEACHER CHARACTERISTICS IN CONTEMPORARY ALTERNATIVE SCHOOLS

Teacher Traits	Public Elementary (5)	Nonpublic Elementary (15)	Public Secondary (6)	Nonpublic Secondary (6)	Nonpublic Combined (8)
At least 3 years' experience	5	6	6	4	6 = 27
Between 1 and 3 years' experience	4	12	3	3	3 = 25
No teaching experience	1	11	0	4	7 = 23
Teacher training	5	14	6	5	7 = 37
College degree but no training	1	7	1	5	4 = 18
Unemployed	0	2	0	0	0 = 2
Children in school	0	3	0	0	3 = 6
Alternative lifestyles	1	10	0	4	5 = 20

and radical lifestyles as much as their counterparts in non-public alternatives. They still adhere to a philosophy based on change within the existing educational system.

Teachers in nonpublic alternatives seem to be less experienced and more inclined to radical social, political, and educational ideas. While most nonpublic alternatives employ some teachers with experience and teacher training, they also hire individuals with little or no teacher preparation or professional experience. In some instances, teachers in nonpublic elementary schools have their own children in the school.

To gain a more detailed picture of the people who seek employment in nonpublic alternative schools, a survey was done of the "job wanted" advertisements in one year's issues of *The New Schools Exchange Newsletter,* perhaps the closest thing to an official organ for nonpublic alternative schools. The advertisements lack a consistent format, but a very general picture can be obtained of the 287 persons who sought some type of nonstudent association with a nonpublic alternative school in 1972. Since the classified "ads" varied in the amount of biographical data included, the figures presented in the survey represent "minimums." "At least" should preface each set of figures. The survey yielded the following data:

Level of preparation

115 applicants possessed some form of valid teacher certification
 55 applicants possessed masters degrees
 15 applicants possessed doctorates
  6 applicants had not gone beyond high school
  8 applicants were college dropouts
  4 applicants were graduate school dropouts

Occupational status

55 applicants just finished some form of schooling prior to seeking employment in an alternative school
48 applicants were quitting a job in public school
12 applicants were quitting a job in college teaching
 5 applicants had been unemployed for a long period of time
11 applicants were leaving a job in another alternative school
 3 applicants were special volunteers from programs such as Antioch's service or work-study internship

Work experience

93 applicants had never taught before
33 applicants had taught two years or less
28 applicants had taught from three to five years
11 applicants had taught six years or more
19 applicants had been college instructors or professors
 5 applicants had been teachers in traditional private schools
34 applicants had taught in contemporary alternative schools
20 applicants had participated in programs such as VISTA, Peace Corps, Teachers Corps, etc.

Living Situation

13 applicants were single parents looking both for a job and a school for their children

34 "ads" were sent by couples seeking teaching jobs together

25 applicants were persons looking for an alternative teaching-learning-living situation, not necessarily a full-time salaried position

The preceding data suggest that teachers in nonpublic alternative schools come from a variety of backgrounds. Many reflect the same discontent with conventional lifestyles as do some younger parents who support alternative schools. Others are experienced professionals frustrated by the slowness with which public institutions respond to the needs of the young. Some men and women are fresh out of college or graduate school and unwilling to make the compromises necessary to work in many conventional school settings. These compromises may range from saying the "Pledge of Allegiance" to giving students numerical grades. The only characteristic, in fact, that is common to almost all people seeking employment in nonpublic alternative schools is a vaguely articulated belief that learning can be relevant, exciting, informal, and child-centered.

Teachers are involved not only in providing alternative forms of classroom instruction but often in creating their own alternative schools. Thirteen of the forty schools in the sample were established through the efforts of a teacher (or teachers) who was dissatisfied with the quality of public education or with his own style of existence.

Historical Antecedents

The composition of alternative schools in past decades generally has obeyed sectarian, class, or ethnic lines. The few nonpublic alternatives that compare closely to contemporary schools in terms of philosophy and pedagogy apparently were made up of students from upper middle-class backgrounds. Schools such as Baltimore's Park School and

Cambridge's Shady Hill School, founded in 1912 and 1915 respectively, were established through the labors of professors from Goucher and Harvard. Allen Graubard argues that schools of the progressive era were "in the main started by professional educators."[4]

Some progressive schools like the Modern School, however, were started by parent groups. In her fascinating story of the founding in 1920 of the School in Rose Valley (Pennsylvania), Grace Rotzel describes how a body of middle and upper middle-class parents acted on their belief in child-centered education. It is interesting to note that the experiences and attitudes of some of these parents resemble those of parents in contemporary alternatives:

> These Rose Valley parents, like many others, were reacting to the rapid changes of the twenties. Changes which had been given impetus by the disillusioning experiences of World War I. Two of the group, for example, had been conscientious objectors, who most certainly were thinking of a better world for their children. Changes were coming to rapidly in communication, in technology, and in science that it was clear that education must adapt.[5]

As for the question of who actually provided the major impetus to progressive schools, Lawrence Cremin concludes,

> No generalization suffices on the question of lay or professional sponsorship. But there is one phenomenon worth noting: except for Manumit and one or two other labor schools, the clientele was overwhelmingly upper middle class.[6]

From the standpoint of history, alternative schools for competent students from middle-class backgrounds have long existed. There were, in addition to a handful of non-public progressive schools during the twenties and thirties, schools which arose in response to new educational philosophies, such as those of Froebel and Montessori. A few utopian communities in the last century fostered alternative schools resembling the contemporary variety. Never before, though, have so many alternative schools of a nontraditional and non-compensatory type existed at the same time. This statement is particularly true of contemporary public alternatives. Is this increase due simply to the numerical growth of the middle class over the past few decades or did certain "unique" factors shape American society in the sixties and early seventies, factors that might compel more parents to seek options to conventional public schooling?

SECTION 2

The
Origins
of
Contemporary
Alternative
Schools

6

Impetus from the Top: The Conventional Origins of Contemporary Alternative Schools

Much of, if not most, educational change has derived from the influence of professors of education, administrators, government agencies, and large foundations. In other words, educational change has been top-down change, change resulting from high-level initiative. Contemporary alternative schools are no exception. Many have come about through the efforts of professionals. In an attempt to isolate the origins of recent public alternative schools, Vernon Smith identifies six impetuses, four of which can be termed "conventional" or "high-level":

1. Educators and administrators, such as Mario Fantini, Dwight Allen, Dick Foster, and Forbes Bottomly, who have been innovators for years and "who now see the development of options as the next step in educational reform."
2. National studies on the status of public education.

3. Governmental and private agencies concerned with social and educational improvements.
4. Community groups interested in upgrading the quality of local schools.
5. Advocates of other reforms who see alternative schools as contributions to the "cause."
6. Students, teachers, and administrators who create their own alternative schools as the needs arise.

Before discussing various conventional impetuses, such as those mentioned in numbers one, two, three, and five, it is necessary to fit the development of contemporary alternative schools into an historical context.

The Growth of Public School Criticism

Though people have criticized public schools almost since the birth of the American common school, not until the progressive education movement did the criticism seriously threaten to alter the very premises upon which public education was founded. In the wake of writings by men such as Dewey, Hopkins, Counts, and Rugg, progressive educators armed themselves with coherent, articulate arguments against conventional pedagogical practices. From World War I until the mid-fifties, the Progressive Education Association (P.E.A.) acted as the official voice of the thousands of professors, school administrators, and teachers who felt that schools had to be child-centered and experience-oriented. Though no better discussion of the movement exists than Lawrence Cremin's history, Otto Kraushaar presents a useful summary of the development of progressive education:

> Progressivism was the main concerted effort to cope with the changing problems that were thrust on the school—and wrought in the school—by wave after wave of immigration, and by the accelerating pace of industrialization and urbanization. It meant broadening the school program "to include direct concern for health, vocations, and the quality of family and community life,"

and beyond that to national and international affairs. It meant "applying in the classroom the pedagogical principles derived from new scientific research in psychology and the social sciences." It meant tailoring instruction more and more not only to the different kinds and classes of children who came to school but to the individual student and his special needs.[2]

The progressive education movement never rallied following the sudden shift in national priorities precipitated by World War II. The P.E.A. officially folded in 1957, but by that time schools already had become absorbed in other matters. A new wave of criticism was generated as many citizens started to examine the nation's educational priorities. Conferences of leading citizens met throughout the fifties in an effort to determine the appropriate responsibilities of the public school.[3]

The fifties inaugurated what Harry Broudy terms a decade of claims that schools were "unresponsive."[4] At first, the unresponsiveness was linked to the country's defense and security needs, especially in the aftermath of the Soviet Union's launching of Sputnik. Broudy contends that the criticism also contained the implication that the advice of leading citizens was not being heeded. James B. Conant argued at the time that professors of education, school administrators, and groups like the National Education Association were not listening to the suggestions of enlightened laymen.

The claims of unresponsiveness continued as the sixties ensued, but the evidence changed. Broudy writes,

> By the mid-sixties the unresponsiveness of the schools was said to be toward the children of the city ghetto, then toward all poor children, and finally toward all children and youth. By the end of the sixties, the schools were alleged to be unresponsive to all social evils—poverty, racism, the war in Vietnam, and the pollution of the environment.[5]

To understand whether these claims of unresponsiveness were valid or not, it is necessary to understand the rising expectations of minority groups, particularly blacks, following the 1954 Supreme Court decision forbidding segregated public schooling. Finding the translation from expectation to reality an uncertain process at best, blacks grew more frustrated and inventive. Some formed "freedom schools" in Alabama and Mississippi. These nonpublic alternatives sought to raise "black consciousness" and stimulate an awareness of constitutional rights. Other blacks abandoned the South for new lands they hoped would provide a more tolerant environment in which to live, work, and educate their children. Joseph Cronin captures the irony of this migration in the following passage:

> During the 1950's and 1960's new minorities fled the farms and flocked to the industrial cities of the North, the Midwest, and the Southwest. Civil rights leaders, inspired by the Supreme Court ruling in 1954 and subsequent government support of their efforts in Little Rock, New Orleans, and elsewhere, sought to open up *de facto* segregated schools in the North. When they moved, they met with the centralized, reformed, reasonably small school boards and their very professional superintendents in these cities. The new minority leaders didn't like what they found.[6]

The reality of *de facto* segregation and racism in the North stimulated a groundswell of black and liberal white criticism of the schools. Books like Jonathan Kozol's award-winning *Death at an Early Age* condemned the racist attitudes which predominated in black schools controlled by white educators. Outbreaks like the one in the Ocean Hill-Brownsville section of New York City served further to dramatize this problem. Studies such as the one completed by sociologist James Coleman provided factual data to indicate that public schools did not assist in increasing the opportunities of most black youngsters for successful, productive lives. The Kerner Commission, formed in the aftermath of the mid-sixties race riots, probed for suggestions to improve the plight of inner city youth. The Commission concluded,

> In an atmosphere of hostility between the community and the schools, education cannot flourish. A basic problem stems from the isolation of the schools from the other social forces influencing youth. Changes in society—mass media, family structure, religion—have radically altered the role of the school. New links must be built between the schools and the communities they serve. The schools must be related to the broader system which influences and educates ghetto youth.[7]

In a similar vein, but regarding New York specifically, the Bundy Panel and several professional consultants called for community boards or other forms of localized boards of education as a step toward involving more members of the community in the operation of their schools.

As more blacks began to press for community control of schools and other institutions affecting their everyday lives, whites started to echo their sentiments. A raft of new books and articles decried the failure of large, factory-like public schools to deal with the needs of individual students. Bigness was bad. Centralized decision-making signaled a fundamental deviation from the course charted by the nation's forefathers. Perhaps no single book of this genre had more of an impact than Charles Silberman's *Crisis in the Classroom*. Here was a moderate layman, instead of a radical educator, saying that the public schools were guilty of "mindlessness." He called on professionals and parents to pay more attention to the handful of innovative programs, such as Parkway in Philadelphia, that promised humane, student-centered learning. Books by John Holt, Herbert Kohl, James Herndon, and others affirmed Silberman's critique, though often in more strident language.

Partly as a result of the wave of criticism—criticism

disseminated to a wide readership through popular magazines, paperback books, and television—an unprecedented public sensitivity to educational problems developed in the sixties. Harry Broudy traces this development, albeit in a somewhat humorous vein:

> Some publishers have done rather well in the late sixties and early seventies with books that called on children and parents to revolt against the schools because they destroyed the child's freedom, creativity, and personhood. In these accounts the blacks were subjugated and oppressed by middle class white schoolteachers; the middle class children were oppressed and depressed by middle class values of middle class teachers; the middle class teachers were oppressed and depressed by middle class administrators, who were part of a middle class bureaucracy.[8]

Though less outspoken than Broudy, former United States Commissioner of Education Sidney Marland acknowledges the unparalleled public discontent with conventional public schooling when he writes,

> When I speak of disrespect and skepticism toward education, I am obviously not speaking in absolute terms, suggesting that Americans no longer have any use at all for the schools and would, if given a free hand, dismiss them altogether as a principal social resource. What I am saying is that there is manifest in this country, to my knowledge for the first time in our history, an active loss of enchantment with our schools. . . . There is a growing doubt about the results of the educational process as it is presently arranged, a lively distrust, fostered by some scholars, as to whether the education process benefits those who experience it. For the first time, Americans in significant numbers are questioning the purpose of education, the competence of educators, and the usefulness of the system in preparing young minds for life in these turbulent times.[9]

It may never be possible to isolate all the reasons why the public schools have sustained so much criticism in the past decade. Some observers, like Harry Broudy, even suggest that public education has not failed nearly as badly as many people would believe. He contends that one explanation for the abundance of criticism is "that for most people discontent is the normal state."[10] Other scholars, however, seem to agree with Christopher Jencks that the American public school has done precious little for many students, particularly those from disadvantaged backgrounds. The public school has been forced to assume more and more responsibilities in recent years—responsibilities ranging from dental hygiene to career education to free lunch programs to the racial integration of American society. Perhaps, too much has been expected of the schools.

Whatever the reasons, public schools have been under attack at least since the advent of the progressive movement. While it is a tenable argument to contend that what people perceive to be wrong actually is wrong as far as the world of everyday life goes, it may be that popular notions of why schools have "failed" are incomplete or unsystematic. For example, few critics of the schools have laid blame on demographic factors. Crowding, however, has placed great strains on existing educational resources, strains sufficient to dilute the high-quality education many middle-class students had been receiving. James Q. Wilson attributes educational problems as well as social disorders such as crime and broken marriages to the rapid increase in the population of the United States since World War II.[11] In 1950 there were roughly twenty-four million people between fourteen and twenty-four years of age. By 1960 the figure stood around twenty-seven million! A veritable "youth invasion" occurred in the United States during the sixties. Wilson concludes, "The institutional mechanisms which could handle problems in ordinary numbers were suddenly swamped and may, in some cases, have broken down entirely."[12]

Whatever the "real" reasons may be, the public schools

have been perceived to be inadequate by a growing segment of the American people. In the critical climate of the sixties and early seventies contemporary alternative schools emerged. It remains to ascertain in a systematic fashion what specific factors contributed to their development and spread.

University Encouragement

Traditionally, universities and colleges furnished much of the impetus for educational reform and innovation. Today, the academic community continues to play an influential part in transforming American schools. Of the forty alternative schools in the author's sample, ten developed as the direct result of efforts by some university-based person or group.

Sometimes the university setting provides an appropriate seedbed for new ideas which, together with the imagination of a few industrious graduate students or a professor of education, stimulate the growth of an alternative school. The nonpublic Mother Sunshine Free School in De Kalb, Illinois, owed its beginnings, in large measure, to the influence of individuals at the nearby University of Northern Illinois.

The World of Inquiry School, a public alternative in Rochester, New York, traces its existence in part to the ideas and grantsmanship of University of Rochester Professor David Elkind. Innovative Adams High in Portland, Oregon, was the creation of Robert Schwartz and six other high school teachers who, in 1967, were completing work at the Harvard Graduate School of Education. As one writer describes their labors,

> They set out to develop a model for a school program that would make possible the achievement of many of the educational objectives that were commonly voiced by educational and social analysis [sic] but had not been established in practice or adequately tested.[13]

Universities also offer more "official" stimulation to contemporary alternative schools. From the days of the Laboratory School at the University of Chicago and the Lincoln School at Teachers College, institutions of higher learning have manifested keen interest in educational experimentation. Recently the School of Education at the University of Massachusetts was awarded a federal grant to sponsor the National Alternative Schools Program (N.A.S. P.). This organization provided teacher training assistance to public school systems interested in fostering alternative schools. In the early seventies N.A.S.P. assisted innovative programs in Pasadena, California, and Marion and Worcester, Massachusetts. It also published literature and operated workshops of interest to educators working toward alternative learning environments.

No stranger to the sphere of educational change, Harvard University oversaw the creation of a prototypical voucher scheme in which parents selected a school for their child and paid his tuition by "cashing in" a waiver based on the local per pupil allotment. The scheme was implemented on an extensive pilot basis in California's Alum Rock School District.

One of the nation's largest Schools of Education is located at Indiana University. Three young professors from that institution were instrumental in establishing in 1970 the National Consortium on Educational Alternatives. Later changed to the National Consortium on Options in Public Education (N.C.O.P.E.), the organization consisted in 1973 of about 400 members. The School of Education at Indiana has underwritten some of N.C.O.P.E.'s expenses, which are used mostly for the publication of a periodic newsletter entitled *Changing Schools* and the sponsorship of workshops. In October 1973 the organization sponsored "the first international convention on options in public education."

Besides providing indirect influence through their graduate students and professors and direct influence through the provision of funds and sponsorship, universities and colleges have assisted the development of contemporary alternative schools, particularly public alternatives, through their education of future teachers. Many teacher training programs encourage prospective teachers to become involved in innovative schools as interns, student teachers, and volunteers. A number of alternative schools have grown to rely heavily on the availability of these volunteers for supplementary instructional purposes. Colleges like Antioch and Goddard, which emphasize undergraduate field experiences and community service activities, supply teachers-in-training and other volunteers to many experimental schools of both the contemporary and the compensatory variety. Indiana University recently inaugurated a nonresident masters degree program in alternative education for people already working in an optional learning situation.

By providing a sanctuary in which scholars and researchers can raise questions concerning American institutions such as the public school, universities and colleges offer an additional, though less direct, prod to contemporary alternative schools. Much of the concern over the possibility that the structure of public schools has exerted a deleterious effect on their functions was generated on campuses by social scientists. They were searching for reasons to explain the apparent inability of schools to aid students from disadvantaged backgrounds. The work of Coleman, Jencks, Katz, and others implies that educational problems cannot be solved simply by introducing more rigorous courses, new instructional strategies, or more staff.

The influence of the academic community on the growth of contemporary alternative schools is typified by the experience of the Cambridge Pilot School. The school originated in 1969,

> ... as a joint effort of the Cambridge School Department and the Harvard Graduate School of Education, two institutions whose relations with

each other were marked in the past by mutual distrust and often by open hostility. Most of the initial impetus came from a small group of faculty and doctoral students at the school of education. This group obtained federal money for the "Training of Teacher Trainers" (TTT) in their proposed subschool....[14]

The new awareness of and sensitivity to the complexity of educational problems is captured in the following description of the project by Robert Riordan, a teacher at the Pilot School:

Like many alternatives, the Pilot School began out of the notion that much of the growing alienation, disaffection, and apathy among high school students could be traced to an irrelevant or culturally biased curriculum and to the impersonality of the public school bureaucracy. It was believed that one way to counteract the problem might be to create a small school characterized by informal human relationships and respect for cultural diversity.[15]

A final way in which some colleges encourage the development of alternative schools, particularly secondary alternatives, is through the loosening of admissions requirements. The Ivy League schools took the lead along with traditionally innovative colleges like Antioch, Goddard, and Oberlin. By seeking students with creative talents and fresh ideas and de-emphasizing test results and grades, these institutions removed one of the primary inhibitions to change in those high schools which cater to competent, middle-class students. There is recent evidence, however, that this trend is being reversed, perhaps in light of the tightening job market.

Encouragement from the Public School Hierarchy

While Paul Mort's now familiar finding that public schools generally change very slowly still seems valid, some changes are occurring. Where they do, there often can be found an imaginative superintendent, principal, or other high-ranking school administrator.

The creation of five schools in the sample can be traced to top-level administrative initiative. Some derived from a desire on behalf of the central administration for a demonstration school that might stimulate faculty improvement throughout the district. In several other cases the superintendent felt an alternative school could solve several pressing problems simultaneously. In Louisville, Superintendent Newman Walker wanted to provide a model center for creative learning, utilize a huge and vacant edifice that once had housed the Brown Hotel, and embark on a positive course toward school integration. The Brown School, an alternative public school covering grades three through twelve, was the answer. Students volunteered to go to the new facility, but quotas were established to ensure racial balance. The ex-hotel was used, and a demonstration center for the development and display of new ideas was created.

The desire to moderate forced school desegregation has stimulated the growth of a number of public alternative schools, though it is often difficult to find a person in authority who admits to such an impetus. Seven schools in the sample derived, at least in part, from the desire to integrate on a voluntary basis. In Tulsa, Oklahoma, the Metropolitan Learning Center was formed,

> . . . to meet a desegregation order at previously all black Washington Senior High School by encouraging white student enrollment. A more flexible schedule and a unique "living cities" curriculum were used as enticements for enrollees.[16]

The Metropolitan Learning Center since has closed, apparently because the spectrum of student interests and abilities was too broad to be accommodated effectively in one setting.

In New Haven, Connecticut, a program similar to the Tulsa center was organized, this time around the theme of the fine arts. One of the underlying motives again was racial integration. In Richmond, Virginia, alternative schools at the elementary, middle, and high school levels were established in an effort to circumvent forced busing and encourage "freedom of choice." Though the "freedom of choice" desegregation plan was struck down by the courts, the alternative schools have remained.

A different approach to the same problem was attempted in St. Paul, Minnesota. With the encouragement and leadership of the central administration, the St. Paul Learning Centers were established. Elementary students now spend part of their day in neighborhood schools and the other part in one of a number of centrally located learning centers. Students from all parts of the city are transported to these centers to visit exhibits, undertake special projects, and mingle with students from other schools.

It is unclear whether the top-level administrators who have helped found these and other relatively radical educational experiments are "career-bound" or "place-bound," to use the argot of educational administration. The desire to build a professional reputation probably is an influential prod to innovate, but the sincere interest of many administrators in creating more responsive learning environments must not be overlooked. Contrary to popular belief, all innovative administrators do not get fired. Superintendents such as Seattle's Forbes Bottomly and Berkeley's Dick Foster are two excellent examples of farsighted chief school officers who have introduced radical changes and lived to tell about them. Newman Walker, presently Superintendent of Schools in Palo Alto, California, epitomizes the forward-looking thrust of these individuals. He expresses his views in the following, straightforward style:

> We think people will work on what they own, on what's theirs. They may not come up with what we want them to, but that's okay, as long as they're aware of what they're doing and its consequences. We're going now for a system of educational alternatives so that people have a choice.[17]

Superintendent Mark Shedd, together with administrative assistant Clifford Brenner and John Bremer, previous superintendent of one of New York City's three decentralized districts, created the Parkway Program and encouraged the development of other Philadelphia alternative schools. Shedd was eventually fired by Mayor Frank Rizzo, but his dismissal was not due directly to his support for alternative schools. Superintendents in other cities have contributed significantly to the growth of alternative schools. Ithaca, New York, and Washington, D.C., are two examples.

Principals, supervisors, and coordinators, in addition to chief school officers, have played a part in stimulating the growth of numerous alternative schools. While teacher unions and associations have been reluctant to endorse public alternatives, the Association for Supervision and Curriculum Development, representing some of public education's middle managerial levels, has encouraged actively the search for optional learning environments.[18] It cannot be assumed, as might be popular, that all administrators willingly sacrifice new ideas for job security and status.

In summary, some members of the public school hierarchy have joined their colleagues in schools of education and assisted in the development of contemporary alternative schools. Their motives vary widely, once again reinforcing the belief that no single factor can account for the emergence of alternative schools. Some professionals view alternatives as the answer to puzzling problems of student motivation. Some see them as an opportunity to forestall forced school integration. Some find alternative schools can double as teacher demonstration centers serving morale-boosting in-service functions for district teachers. Perhaps a handful simply consider alternatives to be an expedient means to gain a reputation, while a few others may find them a "safety valve" to drain off pressure from dissident parents and students.

Corporate and Foundation Encouragement

Since the spread of pauper schools and vocational education in the nineteenth century, business interests have taken it upon themselves to become involved in the realm of education. Sometimes their concern has been philanthropic. At other times it has been purely pragmatic.

Two schools in the sample were aided directly by funds from private foundations. In addition, there are several well-known alternatives that have been assisted by corporations or large foundations. Harlem Prep, one of the most publicized and successful nonpublic alternative schools, received funding from representatives of Standard Oil. This funding was not renewed in 1973, perhaps because the racial tensions that had spurred the initial donations had subsided. Harambee Prep, New York City's pilot public mini-school, started in 1969 with financial backing from McGraw-Hill publishing house. Wingate Prep, a semi-compensatory public alternative high school also located in New York City, was assisted by Pfizer, Incorporated.[19] A grant from the Ford Foundation in 1969 made Philadelphia's ambitious Parkway Program a reality.

Much of the financial assistance from corporations and foundations has bypassed individual alternative schools on its way to organizations seeking widespread educational change. The Ford Foundation funded the studies that paved the way for New York City school decentralization. The Carnegie Foundation sponsored Charles Silberman's research which, in turn, yielded the highly influential *Crisis in the Classroom*. Grants from the Carnegie Foundation, UNESCO, and other bodies helped establish the Center for New Schools. The Center has carried out fifteen experimental programs in Boston, Chicago, New York City, and Washington, D.C. Metro High School, a Chicago public alternative shaped along school-without-walls lines, is one of its best known projects.

Corporate and foundation encouragement of innova-

tions in education can be viewed either as altruistic or as
self-serving gestures. Whatever the case, it is a fact that
most of their funds have flowed to schools directed at an
inner city, disadvantaged, nonwhite population. This fact
can be interpreted as a political maneuver as well as a sincere attempt to redress longstanding inequities.

While many corporations stand to profit from the fact
that better educational opportunities for the disadvantaged
today increase the possibility of a stable future society, one
kind of business interest seems to have enjoyed more immediate benefits. Publishing companies have made substantial
profits from bestselling books that criticize public schools
or suggest solutions to educational problems. Books by John
Holt, Ivan Illich, Jonathan Kozol, Charles Silberman, and
others have topped popular book lists. "How to" volumes on
starting alternative schools, understanding children, and
subverting public education are read, not only by educators
and parents, but by a growing number of students. There
can be little doubt that the emergence of contemporary
alternative schools has been influenced greatly by the unparalleled growth in the publication of literature impugning
the quality of conventional public schools and suggesting
creative options.

Decades ago Upton Sinclair tried to expose the influence that publishers exerted on school policies. He described
a letter written by distinguished educator Charles H. Judd
which told "how the appointment of superintendents in
many cities was in the hands of book companies."[20] While
the influence of these companies currently shows few signs
of this degree of "pull," it is worth noting a recent description of the origins of Chicago's Metro High School:

> Metro was started with impetus provided by the
> Urban Research Corporation, a Chicago publish-
> ing and consulting firm interested in urban issues.
> Urban Research convinced the superintendent of
> schools and several of his assistants that the
> school system should establish Metro and that Ur-
> ban Research could be helpful in getting the school
> off the ground.[21]

Funds from corporate interests almost always have gone to innovations within the public school sector. This fact may appear ironic considering the presence of needy nonpublic alternative schools and the presumed sympathy of private enterprise for independent initiative and competition.

Governmental Encouragement

One of the newest and most influential sources of encouragement for alternative schools is the federal government. Ever since the New Deal, Washington has become increasingly more involved in local educational matters. From the Eisenhower-ordered intervention of federal troops in Little Rock, Arkansas, through the Johnson-inspired Great Society programs, the Office of Education along with the Justice Department and several other federal agencies have striven to ensure equal educational opportunity for students from minority and disadvantaged backgrounds. While the Nixon administration shunned a leadership role in the realm of education, it did endorse a number of innovative educational ideas including alternative schools. Ten of the forty schools in the sample were assisted by some form of federal aid.

Federal stimulation of contemporary, as well as compensatory, alternative schools has assumed several forms, the most prevalent of which are planning, teacher-training, and implementation grants based on the landmark Elementary and Secondary Education Act (ESEA) of 1965. Title I funds from that act encouraged schools to involve parents, nonpublic school authorities, and community leaders in the development of compensatory alternatives. New Hampshire's Lebanon Learning Loft is an example of one such program aided by Title I money. Title III funds were used to establish contemporary alternatives like the St. Paul Open School, Rochester's World of Inquiry School, and Quincy Senior High II in Quincy, Illinois.

Federal funds also have been made available through the auspices of the Office of Economic Opportunity (OEO). Rochester's local educational authority received a grant to study the feasibility of developing an entire system of alternative schools. Development of the Alum Rock voucher scheme was financed by a 1971 OEO feasibility grant. Parents in the scheme received vouchers worth about $680 for an elementary student and $970 for a junior high student. At first, six public alternative schools were set up and 4,000 students enrolled. The number of alternatives and enrolled students was increased the second year of the pilot project (1973-1974).

Besides innovative school projects, OEO funds have been used to establish day-care centers and preschools— organizations which often give rise to alternative elementary schools as the young children mature. Eight schools in the sample started as day-care or preschool facilities, though not all received OEO assistance.

In addition to ESEA and OEO, the federal government, through the Office of Education, instituted the National Alternative Schools Program (NASP) in 1971 and the Experimental Schools Program (ESP) in 1970. Coordinated by the University of Massachusetts School of Education, NASP sought to train personnel to work in alternative learning situations and to provide technical assistance to new schools. The most ambitious and direct action yet undertaken to encourage the growth of alternative schools has been the Experimental Schools Program. ESP at first sought to develop multiple alternatives in three large school districts. The Office of Education solicited "letters of interest from all agencies interested and able to combine into a single, comprehensive, kindergarten through grade twelve project a wide variety of promising practices for 2,000 to 5,000 predominantly low-income family children."[22] In the first year, almost 500 letters of interest were received. Eight planning grants were awarded. On the basis of the plans developed under these grants, three districts were selected to undertake wide-scale educational innovation: Berkeley, California, Unified School District;

Franklin Pierce, Washington School District; and Minne-apolis, Minnesota, Public Schools. The most impressive proj-ect, in many ways, was Berkeley's. At one time over twenty alternative schools existed. Almost half of the city's enrolled students attended these schools by choice. In 1972 three ad-ditional grants were made under ESP. The program later was placed under the direction of the National Institute of Education.*

While federal funding undoubtedly has been the most powerful spur to public alternative schools, other efforts by the federal government have been made to encourage inno-vative thinking. Several "blue-ribbon" commissions have suggested the desirability of alternative schools. The 1970 White House Conference on Children recommended exten-sive federal support for increased educational options.[23] The 1972 President's Commission on School Finance made a similar suggestion, as did an unpublished study of the same year by the Institute for Educational Development. The 1973 National Commission on the Reform of Secondary Education urged, as part of its proposals package, that school districts develop and support "alternative paths to high school completion."[24]

Besides national commissions and federal agencies, many groups at the state level have been active in stimu-lating alternative schools. State Departments of Education in Connecticut, Delaware, Florida, Illinois, New Jersey, New York, Pennsylvania, Vermont, and Washington have given official encouragement to districts and to nonpublic

---

* The most recent involvement of the federal government in al-ternative schooling has come as a result of Teacher Corps in-itiative. Established as a domestic Peace Corps to help improve the quality of education for disadvantaged students, the Teacher Corps currently experiments with new models for pre-service and in-service teacher training. In the tenth cycle (projects funded for 1975-1976), the Teacher Corps divided its projects into five "clusters," one of which concerned alternative schools.

bodies working on responsible alternatives to conventional
public education. One-time Illinois Superintendent of Public
Instruction Michael J. Bakalis, a unique blend of the "three
R's" traditionalist and the visionary, has spoken in favor of
a statewide network of interacting educational facilities
and optional learning environments.[25] Harvey Scribner,
when he was Vermont Commissioner of Education in the
late sixties, helped draft the *Vermont Design for Education,*
a document of educational ideals that might please the most
radical freeschooler. Ewald Nyquist, New York's innovative Commissioner of Education, placed his imprimatur
on a host of alternative educational projects.

Conclusion

All of the so-called "conventional" or top-level sources
of encouragement—the universities, educational administrators, corporations, foundations, and government agencies—have played their part in stimulating the growth of
contemporary alternative schools. Many observers are not
surprised that these powerful institutions and individuals
have been involved in educational change. Joel Spring
argues,

> Since 1900 the power of schooling has tended to
> be in the hands of businessmen, political leaders,
> and professional educators who have been instru-
> mental in the development of the modern corpo-
> rate state.[26]

Harry Broudy contends that the major factors determining
educational policy in the United States are "the Ford and
Carnegie Foundations, the U. S. Office of Education, the
embryonic education industries, and the teachers' unions or
associations."[27] Only the last group has not been an important top-level source of encouragement for alternative
schools. This fact might be attributable to the fact that the
unions and, to a lesser extent, the associations have been
hesitant to share decision-making power with parents and

students. Such sharing of power is a characteristic, as has been seen, of practically all contemporary alternative schools.

It is the argument of this study that conventional or top-level factors alone cannot account for the relatively unprecedented emergence of hundreds, if not thousands, of public and nonpublic alternative schools catering largely to competent students from middle-class backgrounds. Where the influence of government, private business, and administration has been felt most, in fact, seems to have been the sphere of compensatory education.

In addition to and often instead of top-level encouragement, grass-roots elements have contributed greatly to the tremendous growth of contemporary alternative schools in the past ten years. These so-called grass-roots elements include parents, students, and individual classroom teachers—people typically exercising little influence over the course of educational change. It is entirely possible that, even had top-level support never materialized, some contemporary alternative schools would have developed anyway, due in large part to the efforts of these grass-roots groups.

The first International Convention on Options in Public Education, held in late 1973 in Minneapolis, served to dramatize what appears to be a growing rivalry between grass-roots groups and top-level groups over the matter of who will direct the future course of alternative education. At the gathering, many parents, students, and teachers—people who had been working in and struggling to maintain individual alternative schools—confronted those who had organized the convention. They claimed that the major speakers and resource people for workshops were primarily big-name administrators, professors, foundation representatives, and authors. The floor debates that all but replaced the planned addresses demonstrated that a lot of people were upset, not over the fact that the idea of alternative education seemed to have been co-opted by public school systems, but that their labors for the past few years were all but ignored by speakers like Dwight Allen and convention organizers Daniel Burke and Vernon Smith.[28]

Determining possible reasons why grass-roots forces have become more involved in educational innovation during recent years is the focus of the remainder of the study.

7

Impetus from Parents: The Grass-roots Origins of Contemporary Alternative Schools

It is difficult to pinpoint a precise date when the trend toward contemporary alternative schools began. If by the term "trend" one implies a large-scale, coordinated movement of similar bodies, it would be incorrect to classify these schools as such. Contemporary alternative schools account for less than one percent of elementary and secondary schools in the United States. They typicallly exist as independent ventures struggling to raise funds and survive. Taken in the broad context of mounting criticism of conventional public schools, though, contemporary alternatives do share a number of common impetuses. These common impetuses partially justify speaking of the rise of alternative schools as a trend. One very critical factor influencing a great number of alternatives has been increased parental activism.

In his book *Free Schools*, Jonathan Kozol relates a

March 1966 meeting from which emerged a nonpublic alternative school in the Boston area:

> Six years ago, twelve of the mothers and fathers of the children I had known or had been teaching in the Boston Public Schools sat down in a kitchen with me and with my girl friend one night after supper and decided, with us, to begin a little school outside the public system and available for free to kids whose parents had no money. In making that decision, we were very much aware of doing something different and, as we believed, unprecedented in this city and this nation.[1]

Although a handful of freedom schools in Mississippi and Alabama had been set up in the early sixties, the date of this meeting indeed establishes Kozol's New School for Children as one of the first of the recent wave of contemporary alternative schools.

By 1969 several hundred concerned, mostly radical educators were convening an informal conference on free schools in California. Out of this meeting came the New Schools Exchange of Santa Barbara and its newsletter, termed the "first grass-roots national educational reform ..."[2] In the four years that followed the gathering, contemporary alternatives appeared in almost every state of the union and particularly in California, Illinois, Massachusetts, Michigan, and New York.

A New Awareness of the Need for Structural Change

The emergence of contemporary alternative schools has been characterized by an unprecedented degree of constructive parental involvement in their children's educations. Not content to attend PTA meetings or gripe to the local administrator, some parents have created, staffed, and supported schools of their own.

Who are those parents? Usually they are the fathers and mothers of elementary age children. They range in age from their early twenties to their mid-thirties. Many attended college in the mid-to-late sixties, a time of unparalleled criticism of American institutions. Concern grew during that period over the size of the federal government and its failure to respond quickly or effectively to pressing needs. Desires for "participatory democracy" echoed through activist gatherings on and off campus. A growing corpus of literature railed against bureaucratic "red tape" and unresponsive government. When directed at education, these critiques zeroed in on the administrative organization of the schools. Bureaucracy ceased to be a neutral descriptive term during the sixties. To be "bureaucratic" was to be impersonal, self-serving, and amoral in addition to ineffective and wasteful. Why did this intense criticism develop in the sixties?

No single or simple answer to this basic question exists. Certainly schools do not exist apart from other institutions. They exist as reflections of, or sometimes reactions to circumstances in the society-at-large. Allen Graubard feels that alternative schools derive from the same spirit that manifested itself in the civil rights movement.[3] This movement along with the peace movement, the free speech movements on campuses, and other protests of the sixties derived, in turn, from a mounting awareness of the gap between the agencies governing people's lives and the people. It was an awareness many blacks have shared since the days of Reconstruction. Middle-class whites were slow to acknowledge, if not to recognize altogether, their own lack of influence.

Theodore Roszak tries to trace the awareness of individual and minority powerlessness to a series of socio-historical developments following World War II:

> Why and how this generation lost control of the institutions that hold sway over its life is more than we can go into here. The remembered background of economic collapse in the thirties, the grand distraction and fatigue of the war, the pathetic if understandable search for security and

relaxation afterwards, the bedazzlement of the
new prosperity, a sheer defensive numbness in the
face of thermonuclear terror and the protracted
state of international emergency during the late
forties and fifties, the redbaiting and witchhunt-
ing and out-and-out barbarism of the McCarthy
years . . . no doubt all these played their part,
And there is also the rapidity and momentum with
which technocratic totalitarianism came rolling
out of the war years and the early cold war era,
drawing on heavy wartime industrial investments,
the emergency centralization of decision making,
and the awe-stricken public reverence for science.
The situation descended swiftly and ponderously.
Perhaps no society could have kept its presence of
mind; certainly ours didn't.[4]

Possibly the one factor from these postwar developments that contributed most to the rise of contemporary alternative schools was the sense of distrust and apprehen-
sion that came to surround the institutions which existed
ostensibly to serve the public. Discontent was already vis-
ible when Lyndon Johnson's Great Society began to deteri-
orate. The Kennedy-Johnson formula for solving complex
social problems such as widescale poverty and unequal hous-
ing was based on the infusion of massive amounts of money,
personnel, and bureaucratic organization. Referring to the
public repudiation of this policy as the "end of the impossible dream," Peter Schrag writes of the organizational
mismanagement and waste that attended Great Society programs.[5] Roland Barth adds a typical example from the
realm of public education:

The Lincoln-Attucks Program [a fictitious name]
was firmly based on an unfortunate and a very
common assumption: that the unpleasant, and un-
productive, educational experience of children in
school can be rectified by the infusion of *more
money* and *more people*. If a bad educational system exists, saturate it with more of what it already

has: new buses are better than old; new texts better than old; new buildings better than old; what one teacher can do well, three can do better; what two administrators can do adequately, twelve can do better.[6]

Public education in the sixties was swept up in the vortex of several dilemmas. It was expected to ensure equal educational opportunity for all, while simultaneously preserving the individual differences among learners. It was expected to reestablish American scientific preeminence. It was expected to encourage the acquisition of humanistic values and discourage parochial attitudes, while not obscuring the identities of individual ethnic groups. One-time United States Commissioner of Education Sidney Marland admits that "it is easy to understand how people have been led to expect more of education than it can deliver—now or perhaps ever."[7] The commissioner cites a Harris survey of public attitudes toward major American institutions. Conducted in October 1972, the survey showed a drop in public confidence in schools from sixty-one percent in 1966 to thirty-one percent—a thirty point drop in seven years. Marland concludes,

We gain only cool comfort from noting that other great institutions such as medicine, the military, the Supreme Court, Congress, and the press have experienced corresponding tumbles from grace during the same period.[8]

Harry Broudy similarly feels the schools have been caught in a maelstrom that has engulfed other public agencies, including the police, welfare agencies, and public transportation. Public irritation is attributed to the fact that these agencies "clamor for more and more funds, while their deficits grow larger and larger."[9]

The current concern of many Americans with the nature of their institutions seems, however, to reach beyond matters of fiscal responsibility and unrealistic expectations.

Following the lead of an informal coalition of social scientists and journalists, these citizens began to question the desirability of bureaucratic organization in general. Typical of this criticism is the observation voiced by Jerome Murphy that alleged financial problems in state education departments stem more from their form of bureaucratic organization than deliberate mismanagement:

> The nature of the bureaucratic problem in implementing governmental programs has been obscured. Blame has been placed on the inefficiencies of the federal aid delivery system, when in fact major faults associated with categorical aid appear to be general features of public bureaucracies.[10]

In other words, bureaucracies make people err, rather than the reverse.

Great public concern has been directed at establishing some form of bureaucratic accountability. To whom are nonelected bureaucrats actually responsible? Tracking down people willing to assume responsibility for a decision is an exercise in frustration. Nowhere has the search been more intense or frustrating than in the area of American foreign policy, particularly policy concerning United States involvement in Southeast Asia. Determining exactly how a presumably democratic nation could become embroiled, almost inadvertently it would seem, in a devastating war to defend a dictatorial regime has been the focus of attention for scores of historians, journalists, and authors. Many wondered whether government, at local as well as national levels, had outgrown its capacity to represent the desires of large portions of its constituents.

Predictably, the popular discontent with public agencies in the sixties did not pass over the schools. Few institutions are closer to the average American home. Ironically, many of those who seemed most dissatisfied with the structure and the functions of public schools were the same people for whom the schools ostensibly were designed—the white middle class. It was understandable that black parents and parents from other minorities might grow concerned over the cultural bias of the public school curriculum and the unresponsiveness of its predominantly white bureaucracy. It was obvious, though, why white, middle-class parents were discontented.

Origins of the Discontent

The awareness that the institutions serving the public had grown unresponsive and irresponsible was not totally unique to the sixties and early seventies. In his book *The Age of Reform,* historian Richard Hofstadter describes what was one of the first American instances of widespread middle-class dissatisfaction. Focusing on the turn-of-the-century activities of Populists and Progressives, Hofstadter details the rise of powerlessness feelings among the middle class:

> Progressivism, in short, was to a very considerable extent led by men who suffered from the events of their time not through a shrinkage in their means but through the changed pattern in the distribution of deference and power.[11]

Between 1890 and 1910, the typical middle-class citizen—whether a small merchant, professional, or white-collar worker—saw his influence diminish as the power of corporations, interest groups, and unions increased. Hofstadter characterizes the Progressive movement in politics as "the complaint of the unorganized against the consequences of organization."[12] Progressives tried, usually with little success, "to keep the benefits of the emerging organization of life and yet to retain the scheme of individualistic values that this organization was destroying."[13] Echoes of these libertarian strains are heard in the cries recently for student freedom, "free" schools and "participatory democracy."[14]

For all their concern with the trends toward centralization, specialization, standardization, and bureaucratization, the Progressives never developed a viable organizational alternative for governmental agencies, schools, and businesses. Hofstadter concludes that they did not seek to eliminate political machines and bureaucratic agencies, but simply to create cleaner machines and less ineffectual agencies.[15]

Ultimately, as Lawrence Cremin points out, the Progressive movement did exert influence over the schools. The effect was largely technical, however. Few changes were made in the basic structure of public education. The failure to address the issue of educational decision-making might have been the result of World War II. It is a fact that many young people in the thirties were openly critical of American institutions.[16] Their views were quite often similar to those of discontented young adults three decades later. Just as these offspring of the Depression years were graduating from colleges, getting married, and starting families, the war broke out. Thus, at the very point where discontented, middle-class parents were in a position to agitate for school reform, they were absorbed in the nation's wartime mobilization. Young parents in the late sixties were not faced with as extensive or as popular a crisis.

It will never be known for certain if the advent of global war prevented the development of contemporary-type alternative schools in the forties. Many of the criticisms of the schools voiced in the thirties reverberated in the years when alternative schools began to proliferate. Certain conditions in the sixties, besides the less immediate nature of the war in Vietnam, cannot be compared to those of the thirties. The civil rights movement and subsequent pressures for "community control" of local institutions were new. The postwar "baby boom" created an unanticipated burden for all institutions providing services to the young, particularly the schools. An influential group of activist-intellectuals began to write in the late-fifties of the failure of traditionally-respected American institutions.

These and other relatively unparalleled socio-historical developments contributed to growing parental concern with public education—concern that, in turn, contributed to the emergence of contemporary alternative schools.

An Epidemic of Social Criticism

The sixties may well be remembered as the decade when being middle class came to be perceived as a liability instead of an asset by many people. In a retrospective on "the sick sixties" journalists James Q. Wilson and Robert L. DuPont contend,

At the very time when the United States was embarking on the longest period of sustained prosperity since World War II...the quality of life, especially of life in public places, was rapidly worsening. We were achieving the Great Society without producing the good life, enhancing our prosperity without improving our tranquility.[17]

In a similar vein, psychologist Kenneth Keniston observes:

We are approaching, I believe, a new turning point in American society. Despite our growing affluence, despite the triumphant march of technology, despite the inundation of our society with innovations, something is clearly wrong. All the signs are present: our mid-century malaise increasingly shrill cries to "rededicate" ourselves to outworn ideologies which can no longer inspire our commitment, a loss in the sense of social power, and all of the attitudes, feelings, and outlooks I have here called the "new alienation."[18]

Karl Marx also wrote about alienation and related problems, but these were working class maladies to him. In the sixties, middle-class persons were introduced to the possibility that a high standard of living was not the sine qua non of happiness.

Clearly many of the adults involved in contemporary

alternative schools were influenced by the large body of literature criticizing everything from American values to Western culture in general. They read the works of A. S. Neill, John Holt, and Charles Silberman. In addition, they read books like Philip Slater's *The Pursuit of Loneliness* and Theodore Roszak's *The Making of a Counter Culture.* Educational and social criticism often were combined in the same book, as in the case of popular works by Paul Goodman and Edgar Friedenberg.[19]

The recent trend in the social sciences toward scholarly literature that attempts more than a description of existing conditions or a dispassionate analysis of complex social problems traces itself to Gunnar Myrdal's landmark *An American Dilemma.* This immense work pinpointed the discrepancies between the American creed and the American reality by focusing on race relations. As the American reality became clouded with a variety of problems, even as material prosperity increased, scholars started to search for factors that could explain mounting popular discontent. In many cases the search led to the fact of increased bureaucratization—a process epitomized by a corporate economy, centralized government and education, and rule by nonelected "technocrats." Years before Roszak warned of the faults of technocracy, Max Weber, perhaps the world's most famous student of bureaucratic organization, had warned of the possible excesses of such a process. It took, however, the realities of an unpopular war, fiscal mismanagement of social welfare programs, inefficient courts, besieged universities, and similar examples of organizational breakdown to prove the wisdom of his admonition.[20]

In the last ten years a host of widely-read writers have echoed Weber's warnings. Hannah Arendt cautions against "rule by Nobody" or "the rule of an intricate system of bureaus in which no men, neither one nor the best, neither the few nor the many, can be held responsible."[21] As previously mentioned, Theodore Roszak outlines the problems of a technocratic society or a society operated by nonelected "experts":

> In the technocracy, nothing is any longer small or simple or readily apparent to the nontechnical man. Instead, the scale and intricacy of all human activities—political, economic, cultural—transcends the competence of the amateurish citizen and inexorably demands the attention of specially trained experts. Further, around this central core of experts who deal with large-scale public necessities, there grows up a circle of subsidiary experts who, battening on the general social prestige of technical skill in the technocracy, assume authoritative influence over even the most seemingly personal aspects of life: sexual behavior, childrearing, mental health, recreation, etc.[22]

During the sixties, the attention of social scientists was devoted to an unparalleled degree to the organization of American institutions. It has been seen that they began to discuss the effects of bureaucratization on individual behavior. Roszak, for one, speaks of the citizen being confronted by bewildering bigness and complexity and finding it "necessary to defer on all matters to those who know better."[23]

Anton Zijderveld contends that the result of these occurrences has been a pervasive sense of powerlessness. Historically, lack of power was a problem not so much because people previously enjoyed greater influence, but because previously they exerted less. As long as individuals were dominated by a ruler, church, or other agency of hierarchical society, they had no standard of comparison against which to judge their lack of influence. The typical middle-class resident of the United States, however, lives in a society in which he is "partly dominated, partly dominant."[24] In terms of the educational system, this situation means that a parent might be able to exert some influence through informal communication or by voting for budgets, bonds, and board members. At the same time, the parent cannot hope to compete for power with interest groups, teachers organizations, government agencies, or school administrators. Sidney Marland acknowledges the uncertain role of being a parent of a school-age child by drawing from the wisdom of nineteenth century America-watcher Alexis De Tocqueville:

> The evil which was suffered patiently as inevitable seems unendurable as soon as the idea of escaping from it crosses men's minds. All the abuses then removed call attention to those that remain, and they now appear more galling. The evil, it is true, has become less, but sensibility to it has become more acute.[25]

If De Tocqueville's observation is valid, parental unrest over the quality and structure of public education can be traced, at least in part, to a relative increase in lay influence over the schools during the past decade or more.

Typical of the attention currently devoted by scholars to the effects of American institutions on individuals is the work of Philip Slater. In his bestseller *The Pursuit of Loneliness,* he describes the culture in which many parents presently involved in contemporary alternatives lived and went to school. Slater sees college students of the sixties

> . . . leaving an environment in which their attitudes are widely shared and moving into one in which they will be isolated, surrounded, and shunted onto a series of conveyor belts that carry one into the old culture with a certain inevitable logic that can be resisted only with deliberate and perpetual effort.[26]

The factory-like characterization of contemporary society has been applied to schools too. Alvin Toffler argues that "the basic organization of the present school system parallels that of the factory."[27] He further suggests that voucher schemes and pressures for community control are tactics used by opponents of the factory model of organization to "overthrow standardization."[23]

Minority Agitation

Young, middle-class whites not only read the works of activist-intellectuals during the sixties, they watched blacks and other members of minority groups successfully utilize civil disobedience, alternative organizations, and political activism to gain influence over institutions affecting their everyday lives. Foremost in their drive to gain control over their destinies was the effort by blacks

> ... to redirect and reform those institutions that seem to have failed black Americans or, worse yet, have inflicted injury and further disadvantages on racial minorities. In black neighborhoods of large cities, schools have become among the first of these institutions to be challenged.[29]

One of the most publicized efforts by blacks to achieve community control occurred in New York City. Blacks confronted well-organized teachers, led by Albert Shanker, who opposed sharing their control in the classroom. Shanker termed the decentralization of school decision-making that the blacks demanded "an attempt to give a respectable appearance to what is actually a form of cheap accommodation to militants and a cheap solution to social injustice."[30] Blacks and Puerto Ricans, however, were able to gain representation on the decentralized boards of education.

The criticism of public education voiced by blacks was picked up and amplified by many whites. Some agreed that schools were not sufficiently responsive to community concerns. Others echoed the belief that public schools in the United States perpetuated white, middle-class values. These people renounced such values—ones which were perceived to support racism together with conspicuous consumption, imperialism, and other acts of dubious morality. The local school, in the past regarded largely as apolitical, became a potent force suppressing the development of alternative lifestyles as well as nonwhite cultural awareness. As Kenneth Haskins, the principal of Washington, D. C.'s Morgan Community School, argues, a public school system "that fails black children can be tolerated, while a public school system that fails white middle-class children cannot."[31]

The Plight of the Powerless

Their consciousness of institutional unresponsiveness raised by a combination of black activism, disturbing events, and a mounting stack of literature criticizing American society, many young people grew impatient during the sixties and early seventies. Their impatience led to various forms of action—protests, social isolation, alternative organizations and lifestyles.

Many individuals who became involved in establishing contemporary alternative schools interpreted the events and literature of the sixties as indications that average citizens had lost their ability to influence public agencies, schools, and the political system. Though they contributed to an awareness of powerlessness on the part of these people, the events and literature themselves did not *cause* the powerlessness. A combination of sociological and social psychological factors seemed to account for the quite legitimate belief that many young, white, middle-class parents were indeed lacking in effective influence over decision-making processes in the local school, the city government, the hospital, the university, and a host of other institutions.

The first factor was that these people often were transients. Conforming to the prevailing pattern of American life, they moved from place to place. Instead of seeking greater economic security or prestige, though, some sought an idealized community in which could be found freedom from conformity and bigotry and a genuine spirit of cooperation. Others simply were recent college graduates with no particular place to go. The failure of these people to sink roots in a given locality contributed greatly to their feelings of powerlessness. Unwilling or unable to lead a relatively sedentary existence, they rarely were able to build a viable power base.

Second, the people who became involved in contemporary alternative schools often shared radical social views. Together with their general transience, this factor generated feelings of loneliness and isolation. The involvement of many single parents in alternative schools further substantiates their image as havens for lonely, isolated people, people existing outside the mainstream of middle-class America. Parent-operated alternative schools, in fact, could be interpreted as overt manifestations of the need for affiliation and a "sense of community" on behalf of a specific segment of the population. This group consisted of people who often did not support conventional organizations such as the neighborhood church, ethnic club, or union local— organizations traditionally having served as sources of fellowship and political influence.

The search for "community" is a theme present throughout much of contemporary American society. It has roots in a romantic longing for small town society and simplicity, for neighborliness and homogeneity. Today, words like "alienation" and "loneliness" permeate popular writings. Many events of the sixties seem to represent a quest for "community." Demonstrations, boycotts, and other forms of group protest offered opportunities for people of similar convictions to associate on a relatively informal basis while working for social and political change. Communal experiments embodied the desire for closer human relations as well as religious or sociopolitical reform.[32] Protest groups, marches, and cooperative living served to make dissatisfied young adults aware of the possibilities inherent in alternative organizations—organizations existing outside the established perimeters of acceptable behavior. If people could cooperate enough to establish an antiwar group, food boycott, women's caucus, or commune, the implication was clearly that it might be possible to set up an alternative school or day care center.

Several sentences from a pamphlet describing an alternative school in Madison, Wisconsin, capture the longing for and importance of a "sense of community" among the parents who became involved in educational reform during the late sixties and early seventies:

> In this society each family is a self-contained unit, neither responsible nor caring about the lives of others. Children know this. They know that their neighborhood is often a hostile place. As parents we feel isolated, often with few people to turn to in times of trouble or in times of joy. We hoped that in developing the school a community would arise . . .[33]

Similar sentiments are expressed in a description of the development of a St. Paul alternative school:

> It was a complex and painful and joyous process that we went through as we worked out our vision of a school, as we shared our ideas and dreams, and struggled to build a community. Did we want to live communally—shared income—or cooperatively—shared expenses? The subject of communal living kept interferring, then augmenting, then disrupting our conversation about a school.[34]

As the previous passage indicates, achieving the ideal of an alternative learning environment for children sometimes can clash with the establishment of an alternative environment for adult affiliation. More than a few parent-initiated alternative schools have been unable to establish one or the other as a priority—a situation often resulting in the collapse of the school. Occasionally, "second generation" alternative schools will emerge from the ashes of these failures. Six such schools were found in the sample. Each constituted an admission by a group of parents or teachers that a school cannot provide for the learning needs of students and the emotional needs of parents simultaneously. Jonathan Kozol recognizes the same problem in *Free Schools*:

> ... I think it is important to be careful that we do not use the children for the sake of our own egotistic joy in being able to boast to one another of our "wide-open" and "participatory" nature. I tend to be turned off by people and by groups that advertise this kind of claim. Too often, what one finds is that they have superbly "open" and wholly "participatory" sessions, often lasting well past one or two o'clock at night, "relate" beautifully, "communicate" honestly, "touch," "feel" and "open up" to one another marvelously, but never seem to arrive at the decisions that their children's lives and the survival of their school depend upon, grow totally exhausted and end up closing in six months. It seems to me that people who are looking for group therapy ought to find it somewhere else and not attempt to work out their own hang-ups at the price of eighty children.[35]

Not all parents supporting alternative schools, however, seek an avant garde or countercultural variety of community, the kind popularly characterized by frequent soul-baring and searching for new relationships between people. Some parents, particularly those involved in parent-inspired *public* alternatives, simply strive to retain the "neighborhood school" of past years. In some parts of the United States, the neighborhood school has become a euphemism for the all-white, segregated school. Generally, though, parents supporting neighborhood schools are primarily concerned that the distance, philosophically as well as physically, between the school and home be small.

An example of a neighborhood alternative school was the East Hill Elementary School in Ithaca, New York. Faced with a school board decision to close down their antiquated school, residents of the East Hill area bordering Cornell University created enough pressure to keep the school open and to establish it as an alternative learning environment. Parents involved themselves in laying out the school's philosophy, serving as volunteers, and participating in school governance.

Besides their proclivity to resist settling down in one location and their urge to achieve some "sense of community," many parents in alternative schools espouse new attitudes toward family life, marriage, and childrearing. Frequently they acknowledge the need to erase sex-role stereotyping. In fact, nonpublic alternative schools seem to attract a large portion of parents who actively support the women's rights movement and alternative lifestyles. It is not unusual for an alternative school to serve as the springboard for a women's group. A number of the parents who become involved in these schools are mothers seeking a non-domestic identity, but lacking the time, credentials, or opportunity to obtain a full-time salaried position. Harry Broudy points to the beginnings of this trend when he explains, somewhat unsympathetically, that

> ... during the sixties some of the most vitriolic criticism of the public schools came from wives and mothers who had taken an A.B. degree from a "good" college in one of the standard disciplines— a major in history from Radcliffe, a major in English from Smith or Vassar or Wisconsin, Michigan, or Berkeley. In due course the children were enrolled in the public schools and brought home accounts of what went on in the classroom. It occurred to Mother that she could do much better than the teacher, who probably did not have a major in the subject from Smith, Vassar, Radcliffe, or even from a major state university. Later—especially when released from the chores of tending the children—she applied for a teaching position herself, but she was slowed down or

blocked by certification requirements. Among these would be courses in education, which, of course, she had not only not taken, but also would not want her best friends to know if she had.[36]

Colette Dowling provides a different analysis of the concerns of educated mothers and their relationship to the emergence of contemporary alternative schools. Married for nine years and aware of the need for a "chance to grow." Dowling became involved with a group of neighbors in setting up an Upper West Side nursery school. She found the company of the adults in the school "exhilarating" and looked forward anxiously to the informal parent meetings. Most of the twenty-odd families in the Leander Community School consisted of mothers who worked or went to college and fathers employed as professionals. Three-quarters of these families split up during the course of the school's development. Many parents went on to experiment with alternative lifestyles, often involving each other.

It is obvious from reading Dowling's account of the school's growth that, despite the earlier observation, the school *has* met her own emotional needs as well as the learning needs of her child. Describing her involvement in the daily activities of the school, she acknowledges, "In a world where it's so difficult to derive any meaning, there is nothing so gratifying as the immediate human response of children."[37] Add to this need for satisfaction the desire for adult companionship and it becomes clear, once again, that the parent-operated alternative school is often more than an institution for the care of children.

Conclusion

While it is true that parents always have been concerned about their children's education, there is little precedent for the degree of parental involvement found in so many contemporary alternative schools. The fact that these parents were concerned, not only over pedagogical matters, but with the administrative structure of the schools, indicates that a new era of lay criticism of education has commenced.

Initially in the early sixties, black parents sought community control of their schools and other local agencies. Following the lead of the blacks and responding to the disappointing realities of an unpopular war, crisis-torn college campuses, and bureaucratic inertia at various levels of government, many white, middle-class parents voiced alarm at the status of institutions which affected their everyday lives. The emergence of contemporary alternative schools was one manifestation of this alarm.

A misconception concerning these parent-initiated alternatives is that they often served as foci of subversive or leftist political activities. Relatively few alternative schools, however, evidenced more than an ardent reformer's passion for social justice and equality. A handful of schools in the late sixties did embody radical political objectives, though. Ann Arbor's Children's Community School, described in detail in Thomas Powers' biography of Diana Oughton, became a model for revolutionary alternatives, a fact due largely to the notoriety of Oughton (who eventually died in the explosion of her New York City "bomb factory" in 1970) and Bill Ayers (a founder of the school and member of the radical Students for a Democratic Society). In the description of a clash between the interests of black and white parents at the school, Powers observes,

> Black parents were not happy about the situation, either. One reason they were sending their children to CCS was to keep them out of fights. They had, in fact, largely misunderstood the purpose of the school. They had hoped it would be an elite institution which would help their children to get into good colleges so they would be able to find good jobs. Bill and Diana, inclined to feel there *were* no good jobs in America, saw the school as a first step in building a new America where people

would be less prejudiced, competitive and acquisitive. Their indifference to clothes, manners and traditional academic subjects was in sharp conflict with the upward-striving, highly class-conscious black parents who wanted to rise in American society, not remake it.[38]

Rather than radical motives of the classical political variety, a naive desire on the part of young Americans for more options seemed to characterize many parent-initiated alternative schools. This desire reflected a general rejection of anything that smacked of the "Establishment" or conventional lifestyles. Alternatives to the conventional family, marriage, manners, and occupations were sought. The phenomenon of alternative-seeking is recognized by Michael Katz, who writes:

> There are no effective alternatives in American life. This is a realization to which the young came first and older reformers more slowly. The creation of a counterculture and the attempt to find alternatives to public schooling express the same impulse and the same truth. There is only one way to grow up in America if one wants to eat regularly, to be warm, and not to be harassed by the police. For the vast majority there is only one place to go to school, and that place is the same nearly everywhere.[39]

Though Katz neglects to mention it, the conventional public school probably was quite acceptable to the "vast majority" compelled by circumstances to attend it. Whether the relative handful involved in contemporary alternative schools constitute the vanguard of a new social movement or not is difficult to ascertain at present.

The parents of alternative schools, though few in number, do reflect some of the psycho-social characteristics considered to be on the increase among middle-class Americans. They feel powerless to make decisions concerning the institutions that touch their daily lives. They feel powerless because they have lost their roots in the process of searching for the "ideal" community or personal advancement. They feel powerless because they perceive themselves to be isolated from kindred spirits, bereft of a "sense of community." They feel powerless because they *are*, in fact, powerless, having forfeited or lost a great deal of influence as a result of increasing governmental, economic, and educational centralization of decision-making.

Parent-initiated schools thus can be linked to a variety of responses to prevailing and somewhat unprecedented conditions in American society. In part, they represent a response to the need for affiliation and attachment to causes greater than the individual. In part, they are a proving ground for countercultural models and options to middle-class living. In part, they are an outlet for mothers seeking a nondomestic identity and single parents searching for a sympathetic environment. In part, they are an attempt to capture (some would say recapture) the essence of "participatory democracy." In part, they constitute a practical effort on behalf of one-time campus radicals to undermine existing institutions—in this case, the public schools. In part, they represent the almost Promethean struggle of some average citizens to achieve a small degree of control over their own destinies and the destinies of their children.

The contemporary alternative schools that have derived from the efforts and initiative of parents have been shaped by concerns that include but also transcend matters of curriculum, instruction, and philosophy. The concern of these parents, unlike most of their predecessors, includes the desire to reshape the processes by which educational decisions are made and the administrative organization of schools.

8

Impetus from Students:
The Grass-roots Origins of
Contemporary Alternative Schools

As unprecedented as the involvement of middle-class parents in the establishment of educational alternatives has been the recent involvement of high school students in the creation of learning options. Seven of the twelve alternative high schools in the sample were the product, at least in part, of student agitation and imagination. Richard Pratte, for one, sees the rise of student activism in high schools as a major and unparalleled development:

> The major criticisms are no longer outdated curricula, life adjustment, or anti-intellectualism—the basic concerns of the 1950s and 1960s. What is different today is that large numbers of students are exhibiting outrage over their schooling. Many of their feelings—such as their distrust of authority, the irrelevance of classroom talk, and skepticism about textbook learning—derive from

a bitter reaction to American foreign policy, particularly the Vietnam war and the way adults mismanaged it. But obviously the roots of their dissatisfaction are much more complex.[1]

Understanding the reasons why students have become more active in the transformation of their schools is a matter of sociological as well as educational importance.

Campus Spillover

Perhaps the major impetus to high school student activism has been the activism of college students, many of whom were older brothers and sisters of the high school students. The fact that new organizations—be they antiwar groups, underground newspapers and churches, or other protest bodies—appeared on campuses in the sixties suggested the possibility that direct action on the part of high school students might work also.

The first students to press for changes in the conventional public school tended to be young urban blacks and their white supporters. The changes they urged generally stopped short of demands for alternative schools. They wanted an end to curriculum racism, homogeneous groupings, faculties that were largely white, and de facto school segregation. The Parkway Program originated as a response by Philadelphia's central administration to the protests of black students for educational change. In remarks following a January 1967 march by 3,500 black students to the administration headquarters and the subsequent, embarrassing quashing of the demonstration by police, Board of Education President Richardson Dilworth inaugurated a new era in administration-student relations:

There is no doubt in our minds that the students not only have a right to be heard, but that some of their concerns are quite legitimate. . . . Let us stress that in the display of energy and concern witnessed today on the part of high school youth, we saw real evidence of a desire to improve the quality and relevance of education.[2]

The students Dilworth addressed demanded courses in black history and questioned whether their present educations would enable them to succeed in the white world.

As demands by black students began to be heard and heeded, many white, middle-class students started to reassess their own educations. Simultaneously, attempts were being made by a small body of farsighted professionals to make learning more relevant and exciting for students. These efforts were publicized widely, thus increasing the awareness of high school students that educational alternatives did exist. In regard to this kind of mounting awareness of possibilities not previously entertained, Philip Slater observes,

> Revolution does not occur when things get bad enough but when things get better—when small improvements generate rising aspirations and decrease tolerance for long-existing injustices.[3]

The Characteristics of Student Activists

Responding to black protests, campus turbulence, and some "loosening up" in assorted school systems, many white, middle-class students began to express their own disenchantment with everything from school rules to the quality of life in the United States. Lewis Feuer is correct, however, when he argues that discontented students of the sixties, unlike their predecessors in the thirties, are "utterly vague as to the society they propose" or the ideal school in which to learn.[4] Contemporary students have manifested an orientation to specific issues rather than systematic ideologies. Dress regulations, elective courses, and representation on school committees were typical issues around which high school students organized in the late sixties and early seventies. Once a compromise with the school administration had been effected, though, student organizations usually collapsed. No consistent set of beliefs remained to ensure the perpetuation of the groups. In addition, the fact that schools do not host a stable population, but one that constantly changes, undermines any effort to establish a permanent and independent student organization. Where the interest of local teachers and parents has existed, a few student-initiated alternatives have been able to survive. In most cases, however, student-initiated alternatives tend to falter and fail after one or two years. It appears that these alternatives were of great importance to the students originally involved in their establishment, but students subsequently enrolling seemed to lack the vested interest so necessary to sustain these schools as viable experiments. Too often what was an exciting innovation in its first year became a truancy shelter and rest home for world-weary adolescents in its second or third year.

What are the characteristics of the students who originally were involved in establishing contemporary alternative high schools? Except for black students, most of them seemed to share many of the same traits that sociologist Robin Williams detects in his portrayal of the typical college activist of the sixties. This student was more likely than other students

1. To come from families in middle and upper-middle income levels;
2. To come from minority racial, ethnic, and religious backgrounds;
3. To come from urban areas;
4. To enroll in liberal arts programs in social sciences and especially humanities;
5. To take as their role model and self-image the "intellectual" rather than "scientist," "professional," or "businessman";
6. To have less definite career plans and expectations;
7. To attend large, high-quality universities in metropolitan settings;
8. To be exposed to a high volume of political

communication concerning national and international events and issues;

9. To be freshmen, sophomores, transfer students, or "perennial students";

10. Perhaps most strikingly, to have parents who were and are radical or liberal and who in many cases support and encourage their activist offspring. As studies have shown among the Berkeley students, the active left does *not* primarily reflect discontinuity of generations nor alienation from parental values.[5]

It is apparent that many of the students for whom public education seemed to be designed had lost their regard for conventional notions of schooling. The largely white and middle- to upper-middle-class makeup of most contemporary alternatives also suggested that schools were undergoing a continuing division along class lines. Contemporary alternative schools possibly constitute a tacit admission that the goals implicit in crowded urban and suburban schools, with their multiclass and multicultural composition, no longer are acceptable to many young, well-educated white families.

Whence Student Activism?

Explaining why middle-class high school students began to press for alternatives in the late sixties and early seventies is not simply a matter of pointing to campus demonstrations and civil rights protests. As in the case of parental involvement in alternative schools, a number of factors appear to have converged during the years immediately prior to those in which contemporary alternatives emerged.

The combination of an unparalleled increase in the number of adolescents and an equally unparalleled period of prosperity gave rise to a "youth culture," a phenomenon that lacked historical precedent. High school and college students had relatively large sums of money to spend. Perhaps through a media-induced speed-up in social maturation, the "youth culture" came to include new sexual mores, dressing habits, and musical tastes. John Birmingham presents capsulized glimpses of the "youth culture" in his compilation of clippings from high school underground newspapers. The student writers he spotlights in *Our Time Is Now* reflect an amazing degree of conformity in their vocabulary, manner of speech, "revolutionary" ideas, and suggestions for change. Richard Flacks suggests the advent of mass media has tended "to homogenize the content of the youth culture."[6]

The prevalence in alternative schools of students from broken homes and families experimenting with new lifestyles indicates that a "sense of historical dislocation," as Robert Jay Lifton calls it, may have influenced the spread of alternatives. Using the example of the Japanese, Lifton observes that the dislocating process has attended,

> . . . the rapid social change their country has experienced: the feeling that traditional ideologies, styles of group and family life, and patterns of communication are irrelevant and inadequate for contemporary life. . . .[7]

While Japanese youth have experienced even more rapid social change than most American youth, the latter certainly have been made aware of unsettling changes in American family life, public morality, religious habits, and notions of patriotism.

When not influenced by firsthand experience, student awareness of social changes has been stimulated by avant garde publications. The development of an adolescent market for books, magazines, and underground newspapers is one of the most significant aspects of the new "youth culture." Students have enjoyed direct access to "hip," typically simplistic indictments of schools, adults, and society. Through these publications and other media, especially television and movies, students have developed a cognizance of the rights of minors, educational reforms in other places, and the activities of the so-called counterculture. As long as high school students had limited access to this kind of information, they had little choice but to accept the conventional public schools or drop out of school.

The popularization of educational alternatives like Summerhill coupled with the general attack by college students on the "Establishment" introduced the possibility of a third course of action—that of high school students creating their own schools. As long as some adults, either parents or teachers, were willing to underwrite these efforts, local educational authorities in recent years have evidenced a willingness to tolerate such alternatives. Typical of the new, "official" tolerance of student dissent and experimentation is a statement concerning the development of alternative schools in Berkeley, California, made by Larry Wells, director of that city's Experimental Schools Program:

> Credit must also go to the students who persisted in explicating their requirements to an institution historically impervious to change, and as well to the general citizenry of Berkeley who had created an atmosphere open enough, patient enough, and genuinely concerned enough to support the exacting dialogue and inquiry that is the necessary preamble to change.[8]

As in the case of the previous chapter, it is again apparent that contemporary alternative schools, both public and nonpublic, owe their development and proliferation to the labors of more people than professors, administrators, and top-level bureaucrats. Parents and high school students have been instrumental in the creation and support of educational options.

9

Impetus from Teachers: The Grass-roots Origins of Contemporary Alternative Schools

The third major grass-roots group to influence the growth of contemporary alternative schools are teachers. Without a reservoir of dissatisfied teachers and other adults willing to provide instructional services, it is doubtful that alternative schools would have come into existence. It might be disputed that, in this age of militant unions and strikes, teachers constitute a genuine grass-roots group. Historically, though, individual teachers usually have not initiated educational innovations of the magnitude of alternative schools. The picture of the idealistic teacher, stranded in a huge public school and struggling to defend his use of a controversial book or an informal instructional approach, is a popular one. Meanwhile, the role of most of his colleagues is described as that of a "functionary" in a highly bureaucratized system.[1]

Teacher Power

It is safe to say that the impetus behind the growing militancy of teachers' groups also has influenced the movement of many professionals to alternative schools. In an age of civil rights protests and a mounting awareness of administrative arbitrariness, teachers could not help reacting against an institution that determined "whom he will teach; what he will teach; where, when, and for how long he will teach; how he will evaluate the work of students; and (in a measure) how he will teach."[2] Teachers have grown desirous of greater autonomy.

Many teachers, both experienced and freshly graduated from college, have seen in alternative schools an opportunity for greater professional autonomy. Greater freedom can imply anything from rapping with students on a personal level to creating new courses to avoiding any formal observations by supervisory personnel. In a great many instances, however, the desire for autonomy has not been satisfied in alternative school settings. Teachers have traded administrative interference for parental or student interference. Four of the schools in the sample actually were "second generation" alternatives started specifically because the teachers involved became dissatisfied with the format of a parent-cooperative school.

It is understandably threatening for many teachers to confront the possibility that parents might have as much educational expertise as they. In many alternative schools, however, this situation is precisely the case. Because of the large number of college-educated parents attracted to alternative schools, a teacher might find himself disputing educational theory with a college professor, psychologist, or other individual with extensive credentials and impressive training.

Teacher Activists

A significant portion of the teachers in public and nonpublic alternative schools were college students and activ-

ists during the sixties. After graduation some sought gainful, service-oriented employment with a minimum amount
of personal compromise. VISTA, the Peace Corps, Teacher
Corps, Headstart, and other idealistic programs from the
Kennedy-Johnson years attracted large numbers of well-
trained college graduates. The Great Society programs provided extensive training in organizational skills and grass-
roots mobilization. Alternative schools were perceived by
many veterans of these programs as legitimate antidotes to
conventional schools characterized by insensitivity to the
problems of minorities and the poor. Preschools and day
care centers initially were set up. They often gave rise to
alternative elementary schools. Compensatory alternative
high schools also developed as an outgrowth of the poverty
programs and social activism. Two young teachers portray
how their own Bethlehem Community School arose from the
efforts of Great Society workers:

> In early September, Vista workers were assigned
> to the education project at Bethlehem Church.
> Initially they worked at the school from 1:00-3:00,
> the hours the school was open and at the drop-in
> center in the evenings. Emphasis seemed to be
> on drop-in rather than on education. In January,
> credits were to be assigned to the students for the
> work they had done at the school. We, (the Vistas)
> through our fault and the directors fault found
> that we could not honestly give the kids credit
> because of the lackadaisical method of class assign-
> ments and general requirements set up for credits.
> We decided at this point that we had to create a
> legitimate school, with minimum financial aid from
> the church—one that would give the kids legitimate
> high school credit.[3]

Experience in the government-promoted service agencies of the Great Society days provided training in many
skills—including administrative, legal, and interpersonal—
that were quite valuable in the establishment of alternative

schools. In fact, the young workers from these programs could be considered a cadre of seasoned activists ready to become involved in establishing various kinds of innovative organizations.

This cadre of workers had become disseminated throughout the country as a result of their various assignments. When grants and federal moneys were exhausted or tours of duty completed, other employment had to be found. Many of the white, middle-class men and women involved in the programs had grown frustrated by their inability to make significant dents in local poverty. Others felt uneasy about their lack of acceptability to non-middle-class residents of barrios, slums, urban ghettos, reservations, and mountain hollows. Radicalized to their own upbringing but unable to blend into a different socioeconomic situation, the young workers typically manifested uncertainty about their future roles in society. Alternative schools served as "halfway houses" assisting many of them in their readjustment to middle-class society. From their alternative school experiences, they either moved on to graduate school and conventional employment or rejected mainstream America and sought new lifestyles.

The number of teachers (with or without experience in Great Society and related programs) who have grown disenchanted with American society has been great in recent years. Some have felt that little could be done to effect widespread changes in "the system." Others came to hold the belief that schools could figure directly into the process by which society would be transformed. One type of teacher activist, symbolized by Jonathan Kozol, has striven to ensure an equal educational opportunity for underprivileged youth while simultaneously seeking institutional alternatives appropriate to a new society. Kozol sums up his attitude in *Free Schools*:

> The public-school affiliated ventures . . ., such as Parkway School in Philadelphia or Morgan School in Washington, D.C. may constantly run skirmishes

on the edges of the functions and priorities of do-
mestication; in the long run, however, they cannot
undermine them. The school that flies the flag is,
in the long run, no matter what the handsome community leader in the startling Afro likes to say,
accountable to that flag and to the power and to the
values which it represents. This is, and must remain, the ultimate hang-up of all ventures which
aspire to constitute, in one way or another, a radical alternative "within the system."[4]

Another group of teacher activists have concentrated
on alternative schools attracting largely white, middle-class
students. In an attempt at consciousness-raising among this
group of students, they have stressed such activities as re-
nouncing materialism, developing alternative decision-making processes by which to govern schools, and creating utopian prototypes.

It remains to be seen whether contemporary alternatives or any schools, for that matter, can occupy the vanguard of social change movements. A careful reading of the
history of successful revolutions does not find schools play-
ing this kind of leadership role. Schools, other than boarding
schools, must coexist on a daily basis with many other organizations in society. They do not seem well-suited to the
rigors of revolution. In places where successful revolutions
have occurred—for example, in the United States, the
People's Republic of China, and Cuba—alternative economic,
military, and political organizations have been instrumental
in preparing the participants for a new social order. Schools,
per se, tended to develop only after the old order had been
supplanted.

Many teachers have avoided being identified as political
radicals, though they sympathized with or saw themselves as
members of the counterculture. For them, the alternative
school constituted as much a new style of community interaction as an experiment in learning. A portion of this group
are teachers in their thirties and forties searching for al-

ternative lifestyles as well as schools. As with the ex-Great Society workers, these teachers often utilized the alternative school as a halfway station between their former lives in conventional schools and a radical career change, communal venture, or other shift in living pattern.

The availability of college graduates willing to work in alternative schools for relatively low wages and little job security is another factor contributing to the spread of contemporary alternatives. This group's existence might be linked to the absence of risks in conventional employment opportunities. There is nothing mundane or routine about most alternative schools. The work has been described by those involved as exhilarating, exhausting, and rewarding. Alternatives typically afford an opportunity for teachers to feel direct responsibility for the very survival of the schools—a feeling available in few conventional public schools.

Voluntarism

Volunteers represent an additional source of teaching personnel for public and nonpublic alternative schools. Without parent volunteers, college students, student teachers, and community resource people, many low-budget alternatives would be unable to provide the individualized instruction and personalized attention on which they pride themselves.

Voluntarism certainly is nothing unique to contemporary alternative schools. Volunteers have been involved in education at least since the nineteenth century. There are, however, several distinct types of voluntarism:

1. *Philanthropic voluntarism.* Characterized by an interest solely in the continuation of the service organization, this form of voluntarism often involves the well-to-do and parents, particularly mothers, of grown children.
2. *Exploratory voluntarism.* Volunteers seem to be sampling a new occupation or working through

transitory personal problems as much as they are
providing a charitable service. Volunteering,
because it involves no contract or salary,
constitutes a minimal commitment, one permitting
relatively easy access and departure.

3. *Sociable voluntarism*. This form of voluntarism is
motivated by a desire to locate companionship and
comfortable surroundings as well as to provide a
charitable service.

In the past, most voluntarism in education appears to
have been of the philanthropic variety. While little reliable
data exists to substantiate the claim, the years since World
War II seem to have been characterized by an increase in
the number of volunteers motivated by factors other than
charitable service and pure altruism. This increase might
be traced to an overabundance of college graduates. With
millions of young adults having gone to college because it
was "the thing to do" and a general decline in the attrac-
tiveness of traditional careers such as business and industry, a large pool of educated labor has been created. These
people have tended to look for employment that was rewarding psychologically as well as, or instead of, financially. The
rejection of traditional materialistic incentives might be related to the fact that many recent graduates have been sub-
jected to accounts in the media and from their parents of the
short-comings of affluence. Many now choose to spend their
twenties in a state of voluntary poverty sampling various
occupations, pursuing graduate degrees, or working out
personal problems. Volunteering to work in an alternative
school has served as an important experience for many of
these unsettled and uncertain young adults.

The increase in the number of married and single
mothers seeking nondomestic activity, but lacking credentials for stimulating and salaried employment, also contributed to the current popularity of "exploratory voluntarism." "Sociable voluntarism" similarly has characterized
this group of women as well as many male volunteers. Alter-

native schools along with consciousness-raising groups, food cooperatives, underground churches, and similar informal groups have provided settings in which to associate with adults in similar situations and satisfy the need for meaningful employment.

Conclusion

As in the case of parents and students, teachers have been attracted to public and nonpublic alternative schools for a variety of reasons. The rising rate of unemployed teachers—largely the result of overproduction of teachers in the sixties and declining school enrollments—probably has accounted for some of their interest in these new schools. The increase, or at least the surfacing, of teachers desiring autonomy and greater job satisfaction more than higher salaries and job security also has been a factor in the popularization of contemporary alternative schools. Many of these teachers perceived teacher unions and associations as relatively conservative, self-serving groups more concerned with professionalism than pupils. Another factor has been the development of cadres of well-educated individuals who gained experience during the sixties in social service programs and who sought other "relevant" employment as they outgrew or had to leave their positions. The increase in the availability of well-educated volunteers has been an additional factor in the emergence of contemporary alternative schools.

10

The Retransformation of the School

The emergence of contemporary alternative schools points to several major developments in American society as well as American education. First, contemporary alternatives constitute as much a challenge to the bureaucratic structure of public institutions as to their goals and methods. Up until the mid-sixties critics of the schools had never zeroed-in on the administrative organization of individual schools. Issues like community control of schools had not been probed seriously since the turn of the century. For the first time, parents and students became involved in the planning and operation of schools. Interviews with parents indicated that many had become dissatisfied with their relative powerlessness vis-à-vis the conventional public schools to which they sent their children.

A second significant aspect of contemporary alternatives is their composition. Made up largely of capable white students from liberal middle-class families, these schools seem to signify growing unrest among a segment of the population that had once been among public education's staunchest supporters. No longer are alternative schools the privilege of the wealthy, the choice of the sectarian, or the lot of the handicapped and the disadvantaged. The overcrowding of public schools and the apparent shift in their priorities that has accompanied the enrollment of more students from disadvantaged backgrounds seems to have influenced this disaffection. Other factors, of course, have been at work also. Along with the increased sensitivity to middle-class powerlessness mentioned earlier, shifts in the structure of the family and attitudes toward childrearing have contributed to the growth of alternative schools. It is still difficult, however, to understand exactly how these factors have shaped the development of alternatives.

Harry Broudy suggests a third important aspect of the rise of contemporary alternative schools. He contends that public education has fallen victim lately to a general lack of leadership—much as has been the case with American politics in the wake of the Watergate crisis:

> Can one blame the public for turning to journalists and the foundations for guidance on the public schools? As a matter of fact, do not the professional organizations like the American Educational Research Association and the American Association of Colleges for Teacher Education invite these laymen to their annual conventions to hear "wholesome criticism," and perhaps to find answers that they themselves cannot produce? Can one blame the black community or the Eastern intellectuals or the red-neck communities for demanding control of their own schools? Society abhors a vacuum of authority; today all sorts of bids for authority in education are being sucked in to fill that vacuum. The polite words for this chaos are "alternatives" and "cultural pluralism."[1]

Whether this "vacuum of authority" is the legacy of over-bureaucratization or not remains to be determined. While bureaucratization does not automatically mean poor education or poor government, it does bespeak a shift in the locus of control from the citizenry or the consumers to the "technocracy" and the producers. It is likely that grass-roots movements do not thrive where centralized authority is respected and firmly in control.

Many of the factors accounting for the emergence of contemporary alternative schools have been present before. Criticism of the public schools is not unique to the past decade. The thirties witnessed a growing number of people who questioned the fundamental purposes of the schools as well as the society. Harry Broudy and John Palmer maintain that similar inquiries attend any period in which "the roads to success" become obscured.[2] There have existed isolated experimental schools and countercultural organizations since the utopian movements of the past century. Yet, with some assurance it can be argued that these progressive schools and experimental ventures never existed in such abundance as they do currently. It is the confluence of many factors—a burgeoning student population, an unpopular war, civil rights activism and the establishment of freedom schools, the women's rights movement, a decade of hollow prosperity, and a leadership and knowledge vacuum in education—rather than any single unprecedented event that appears to underlie the emergence of hundreds of public and nonpublic alternative schools since 1965.

The Current Status of Contemporary Alternative Schools

The data on which the forty-school study was based were collected and analyzed between 1972 and 1973. In the years that have followed, several developments have affected the spread of contemporary alternatives. The national economy has undergone a period of rising inflation and subsequent recession. The idea of alternative schooling has been co-opted by individuals and groups whose interests often differ substantially from those of people involved in earlier experiments. Finally, "hard data" on how well alternative schools educate students have begun to be gathered largely as a result of formal evaluations of externally-funded public alternatives. Each of these developments will be discussed briefly.

Economics. It is impossible to determine how many alternative schools have been closed or have failed to open as a direct result of recent fiscal crises. People involved in alternatives are quick to comment on the monetary Sword of Damocles ever poised over their heads. They are equally quick, however, to note that alternative schools are designed to cost no more than conventional public schools. In fact, many nonpublic alternatives function much more inexpensively than conventional public schools.

Proposals for externally-funded alternative schools typically include statements to the effect that operational costs will be governed by the local per pupil expenditure. The widely-publicized Alum Rock Voucher Project has demonstrated that a school district can offer multiple alternatives (at the pre-high-school level) without increasing per pupil costs.[3] Unfortunately for those who regard voucher schemes as the economic salvation of the alternative school "movement," districts have been reluctant to follow in Alum Rock's footsteps. Recently, East Hartford, Connecticut, voted down a voucher plan that would have been supported financially by the National Institute of Education. East Hartford school principals lined up solidly against the plan. Denis Doyle, Division Chief of N.I.E.'s School Finance and Organization Division, has been quoted as saying that the "steam has gone out of it [voucher plans]" and the federal government "just doesn't seem to care about it" any longer.[4]

Despite the uncertain economy and the seeming failure of vouchers to take root outside of Alum Rock (San Jose), alternative schools continue to operate. In some districts,

alternatives have been created at the same time that cuts
have been made in staff and services. Many of the new crop
of alternatives, however, are three-R schools that stress discipline, basic skills, and respect for authority.

Co-optation. One reason why alternative schools have
weathered recent fiscal maelstroms is the fact that they
have been adopted by individuals who did not support them
originally. Intended as ends in themselves by early adher-
ents, alternative schools increasing are being exploited as
means to such goals as "back-to-basics" learning and neighborhood (segregated) schooling. The furor over busing
students to achieve racial integration has produced a host
of suburban nonpublic alternatives. Public systems have
created magnet schools, learning centers, and freedom-of-
choice plans in an effort to forestall court-ordered busing.
It is still unclear what proportion of the anti-busing group
is involved in the "back to basics" movement, but conservative alternatives, with their dress codes and drill, seem to
attract an unusually large number of white, middle-class
students.

Other individuals have used alternative schools to advance special interests. Some blacks and Chicanos see alternative schools as opportunities to strengthen ethnic identity. The demise of tax-supported Black House and Casa de
la Raza in Berkeley may have dampened the hopes of those
who wish to pursue ethnicity within the "system," but the
issue of ethnic schools is far from dead.[5]

Lawrence Kohlberg and his co-workers at Harvard have
established a "just community" high school in Cambridge to
test Kohlberg's theories of moral development. He explains
the mission of the school thusly:

> We have stated the theory of the just community
> high school, postulating that discussing real-life
> moral situations and actions as issues of fairness
> and as matters for democratic decision would stim-
> ulate advance in both moral reasoning and moral

action. . . . Most alternative schools strive to establish a democratic governance, but none we have observed has achieved a vital or viable participatory democracy.[6]

Another boost to the cause of alternative schooling has been provided in the reports of several recent blue-ribbon commissions charged with recommending ways to improve public secondary education. In a review of suggestions made by the Office of Education's National Panel on High School and Adolescent Education, the Kettering Commission, and the President's Panel on Youth, A. Harry Passow notes that there is almost unanimous support for the expansion of alternative schools and optional learning programs as antidotes for declining academic achievement and diminished student interest in school.[7]

Research on alternatives. The last three years have witnessed an increasing (though still very small) number of systematic studies of alternative schools. A survey of the ERIC *Current Index to Journals in Education* indicates that 158 articles on alternative schools appeared between January 1973 and May 1976. While only a fraction of these articles represent actual research, it is apparent that those who are interested in alternative schools can now obtain some idea of the problems encountered in establishing and maintaining such enterprises and in assessing their effectiveness.

Much of the recent research has focused on organizational aspects such as how decisions are made and who makes them. This fact supports the contention of the present study that the structure of contemporary alternative schools is as important an element in understanding their growth as their goals or pedagogical characteristics. Four studies have appeared that try to account for the success or failure of alternatives in terms of organizational factors.[8] Both Terrence Deal and Bruce Cooper see alternative schools as organic entities moving through distinct stages of development. Organizational immaturity as symbolized by disagreement over school goals and lack of sophistication in group process is found to be the cause for the demise of many alternatives. Chris Argyris contends that alternative school advocates' "theories-in-practice" (as opposed to their "espoused theories") are little different from the beliefs of the "hard-hats" they seek to condemn. As a result of this unconscious hypocrisy, decision-making in alternative schools frequently bogs down amidst conflicts between abstract, idealistic aims and pragmatic inclinations bred of middle-class upbringing. Steven Singleton and his associates find that the alternative school they studied failed because of (1) ambivalence concerning whether students or teachers should initiate changes, (2) fear of assertive leadership, (3) disagreement over the value of academic pursuits, and (4) the general absence of critical dialogue.

In addition to the handful of competent research studies, the recent literature dealing with alternative schools includes at least a half dozen evaluations of externally-funded projects involving alternatives. As a collection of data, the evaluations do not constitute an overwhelming mandate for or against alternative schools. The evaluations differ greatly in design, execution, quality of analysis, and sometimes results.

Two University of Oregon evaluators find that students who attended an urban public secondary alternative improved in their attitudes toward studying and teachers, but not in their academic achievement.[9] Ralph Nelsen, on the other hand, writes that FOCUS, a school-within-a-school for one-hundred disaffected students from Portland, Oregon, has succeeded in 1) lowering absenteeism, 2) improving student self-concept, and 3) raising achievement in reading, composition, and mathematics.[10] Similarly positive results are reported by Edsel Erickson and Michael Walizer in separate evaluations of alternative schools.[11] Drawing on the RAND evaluation of the Alum Rock voucher schools, Jim Warren observes that some of the greatest benefits of the project have derived from changes in teachers, rather than students.[12] He notes that teachers feel more positively about their work, collaborate more on instructional planning, and determine more of the allocation of school resources. Despite these encouraging findings, Warren does not indicate that they have led to dramatically increased student achievement or demonstrably greater success than Alum Rock's non-voucher schools.

It is impossible to generalize from the evaluations of alternative schools that students do better or worse than they would have done in conventional settings. Much of the data is based on self-reports and personal interviews. Evaluators often apologize for the conditions under which data was collected. No uniform set of tests were used in the schools subject to external evaluation. Some evaluations neglected to provide control group data. Follow-up studies to determine what happens to graduates of alternative schools have not been attempted.

The future. Since the forty-school study was completed, alternative schools have gained in respectability. With the disappearance of most of the shoestring operations and radical free schools, the general public as well as the mainstream of the education profession have been more willing to embrace the concept of optional learning environments. At the same time, external and internal pressures remain to cloud the future of contemporary alternative schools.

Regarding external factors, alternative schools have yet to receive the unqualified endorsement of either the National Education Association or the American Federation of Teachers. Interest in voucher schemes and public support for private education, each of which could advance greatly the cause of alternative schooling, shows signs of slackening. Fear continues to exist among civil rights activists that alternative schools will be used to shelter segregationists.

The failure of many alternative schools to demonstrate dramatic increases in student achievement also has contributed to the failure of a ground swell of support.

Declining school enrollment may pose additional problems. Earlier in the book it was argued that contemporary alternatives derive, in part, from the unparalleled growth in school-age population during the sixties. Large numbers meant crowding, and crowded classrooms generated complaints about impersonal treatment and ineffective teaching. Advocates of alternative schools promised smaller schools and more personalized attention. With the school-age population declining markedly, it may be more difficult to use these justifications in the future.

Another external factor, one related to the previous example, concerns the centralization of schooling in the United States. At first justified on the basis of efficiency and later because of the need to integrate, the movement to consolidate school districts and schools has been growing since the first part of the century. Educators now entertain visions of huge, college-like campuses centrally located in large urban areas and accessible by mass transit. It is questionable whether the notion of small, intimate alternative schools can withstand such a trend.

A final external factor involves the end of the Vietnam War, the quieting of civil rights activism, and the general abandonment of social causes by young adults. Current social apathy and self-concern has sapped the alternative school "movement" of much of its driving force. Financial security has replaced more idealistic interests among teachers and parents who once counted themselves in the vanguard of social change. Women no longer need to attach themselves to alternative schools to establish nondomestic identities. The preceding developments have had the cumulative effect of eliminating much of the original alternative school constituency. Support from public school systems has served to stabilize many alternative schools for the moment, but the history of educational change suggests that innovations which do not expand soon wither.

Not only are alternative schools subject to outside forces, they must cope with a host of internal problems, including the maintenance of staff and student morale. Existing on "soft money" or uncertain tuition payments for long periods of time can be enervating for all involved in the operation of an alternative school. Equally de-energizing can be the effort to build a stable instructional program around volunteer help and parent egos. In some instances, the imperative to keep coming up with new ideas, implicit in so many experimental ventures, results in the premature scrapping of decent programs and the mental exhaustion of dedicated teachers. Finally, the sheer amount of work necessary to operate an alternative school can lead to "burn out."

The impact of these internal and external factors may be to retard the growth of new alternatives and hasten the demise of existing ones. The sacrifice in terms of time, energy, and emotions may not be worth it. Yet, as long as researchers are unable to determine the one best way to educate all students, the concept of alternative schooling will remain credible. Until consensus is reached that all schools should strive to inculcate the same values, alternative schools will find supporters.

Transcending the status of an educational fad is probably the most pressing problem within the alternative school "movement." In order to accomplish this task, some people argue that alternatives must dissociate themselves from the broad social developments from which they partially derive. Others, antithetically, feel that the ultimate hope for alternative schools rests squarely on their willingness to identify with issues of society-wide significance. Robert Riordan concludes:

> Alternative schools must see themselves as part of
> a network of other mutually supportive institu-

tions, including not only other alternative schools, but day-care centers, storefront counseling centers, food cooperatives, political action groups, and other alternative and counterinstitutions as well. It does not make much sense to view yourself as an alternate institution unless you can envision an alternative world, and work to bring it about.[13]

Whether they eventually link up with innovative social and political developments or remain limited educational experiments, contemporary alternative schools constitute a retransformation of the institution that inducts most of America's youth into adult society. The original transformation resulted from the impact of progressive education on American schools. It is still too early to tell if the retransformation will have more of an effect than the transformation. Skeptics hold that neither are robust enough to alter the basic assumptions undergirding schooling in the United States.

Addenda

Public Elementary Schools (29)—5
   John B. Cary School, Richmond, Virginia
   East Hill Elementary School, Ithaca, New York
   P. S. 191, New York, New York
   Welsh Elementary School, Rockford, Illinois
   World of Inquiry School, Rochester, New York

Nonpublic Secondary Schools (40)—6
   Baltimore Experimental High School, Baltimore, Maryland
   Milwaukee Independent School, Milwaukee, Wisconsin
   The New School, Washington, D. C.
   The New School Workshop High, Portland, Maine
   Palfrey Street School, Watertown, Massachusetts
   The Unschool of New Haven, New Haven, Connecticut

Public Secondary Schools (38)—6
   Alternatives East, Wyncote, Pennsylvania
   The Brown School, Louisville, Kentucky
   Homebase School, Watertown, Massachusetts
   School for Human Services, Philadelphia, Pennsylvania
   School without Walls, Washington, D. C.
   Woodlawn Program, Arlington, Virginia

Nonpublic Combined Elementary-Secondary Schools (53)—8
   Akron Free School, Akron, Ohio
   Climbing Tree, Comstock Park, Michigan
   Community School, Salem, Virginia
   Community School of Philadelphia, Philadelphia, Pennsylvania
   The Forum School, Washington, D.C.
   Free School, Oak Park, Illinois
   Michaels Community School, Milwaukee, Wisconsin
   Warehouse Cooperative School, Roxbury, Massachusetts

INTERVIEW SCHEDULE FOR A STUDY OF
CONTEMPORARY ALTERNATIVE SCHOOLS

   I.   Educational Goals

      (Q1)   *Which of the following types of goals generally
             characterize your school?*
             Exploratory goals—Characterized by many student-
             initiated activities, project learning, stress on

creativity and natural growth, and terms like
"open education."
Preparatory goals—Characterized by career
education, vocational training, acquisition of basic
reading, writing, and arithmetic skills, and
preparation for socially acceptable targets.

Revolutionary goals—Characterized by ideological
commitments, radical curriculum content, and
preparation for targets that are not acceptable to
the general population.

Participatory goals—Characterized by a dedication
to democratic school government, town meetings,
and student decision making.

Therapeutic goals—Characterized by stress on
self-exploration, group process, personal growth,
and affective development.

Academic goals—Characterized by unusual courses,
college-style learning experiences, seminars, and
student independent study.

Demonstrative goals—Characterized by emphasis on
the school as a lab for the development of new
techniques, teacher training, and educational
experimentation.

No primary goals.

II. Pedagogical Dimensions

(Q2) *How is age-grouping accomplished in your school?*
Grades corresponding to chronological years.
Mixed-age units of two or three years.
No age-grouping at all.

(Q3) *How is ability-grouping accomplished in
your school?*
Students are grouped heterogeneously.
Students are grouped homogeneously.
Students are grouped homogeneously on a limited
basis (i.e., in reading only).

(Q4) *How is instructional grouping accomplished in your school? (Only indicate that mode(s) which is used frequently)*
Large-group instruction.
Small-group instruction.
Individualized instruction.
Independent study.

(Q5) *How is the curriculum structured in terms of required and elective courses?*
Elementary level—No requirements.
　　Requirements in reading and mathematics only.
　　Additional requirements.
Secondary level—No elective courses.
　　Some electives.
　　All electives.

(Q6) *How do the curricular offerings compare to those in a conventional public school?*
Generally equivalent.
Less variety.
More variety.

(Q7) *Which of the following instructional features can be found in your school?*
In-and-outness (extensive use of extra-classroom environments).
School-without-Walls.
School-within-a-School.
Learning centers.
Creative room arrangement.
Work-study program.
Simultaneous use of various learning materials.
Integrated day (undivided by specific periods).
Modular scheduling.
Multiple staffing.
Team Teaching.
Cross-age tutoring.

(Q8) *How can teacher-student relations be characterized in your school?*
Professional (formal, superordinate-to-subordinate).
Parental (informal, superordinate-to-subordinate).
Democratic (informal, as equals).

(Q9) *What are the bases for evaluation of student progress in your school?*
Standardized tests.
Fixed scales and grades.
Individualized judgments of performance.
Criterion-referenced measures.
No consistent form of evaluation.

(Q10) *How is student progress reported in your school?*
Report cards.
Portfolios of student work.
Parent-teacher conferences.
Student-teacher conferences.
Parent-teacher-student conferences.
No method of reporting progress.

III. Administrative Organization

(Q11) *How would you characterize the administrative organization of your school? (Choose only one)*
Parent cooperative.
Parent-teacher operated.
Parent-teacher-administrator operated.
Teacher-administrator operated.
Headmaster operated.
Teacher operated.
Student operated.
Student-teacher cooperative.
Student-teacher-administrator operated.

(Q12) *Which of the following decision-making roles or processes or groups exist in your school?*
Town meeting.
Committees.
Faculty meetings.
Advisory groups.
Elected Board of Trustees.
Appointed Board of Trustees.
Coordinator.
Headmaster or director.
Autonomous teachers.
Teacher planning teams.
Consultants.

IV.   Composition

(Q13) *What is the estimated educational background of the*
students in your school? (You can choose more
than one)
More than 25% with successful previous
experience in conventional public schools.
More than 25% with unsuccessful previous
experience in conventional public schools.
Some students with nonpublic school experience.
Students with day-care or preschool experience.

(Q14) *Which of the following characteristics best fit*
the parents of the students in this school?
50% or more from intact families.
50% or more middle class.
25% or more working class.
25% or more upper-middle or upper class.
50% or more white.
25% or more nonwhite
25% or more working mothers.
25% or more engaged in new lifestyles.
25% or more new residents in the community.
50% or more with liberal political beliefs.
25% or more professionals (at least one in the
family).

(Q15) *Which of the following characteristics best fit the*
teachers in this school?
At least 3 years of teaching experience.
Between 1 and 3 years of teaching experience.
No teaching experience.
Teacher training courses in college.
College degree but no teacher training courses.
Unemployed just prior to getting the present job.
Children of teacher in the school.
Teacher engaged in alternative lifestyles.

V.   Impetuses to the Development of Alternative Schools

(Q16) *Which of the following factors influenced the*
emergence of this alternative school?
Desire for improved instruction.
Desire for a different curriculum.

Tense racial situation.
Threat of forced school integration.
Federal grants.
State grants.
Private grants.
Student discontent in local public schools.
Closing of an existing alternative school.
Threat to close an existing public school.
Need for day-care facilities.
Availability of unused building facilities.
Desire for a "neighborhood school."
University influence.
Second generation alternative school arising out of dissatisfaction with previous alternative school.
Offshoot of a social service program.
Influence of a commune or collective.
Teacher frustration in local public school.
Other: (Please specify).

Notes

Chapter 1 Why Look at Contemporary Alternative Schools?

1. The author is indebted to Gordon Van Hooft, Acting Director of the Division of Secondary Supervision, New York State Education Department, for this remark concerning Ewald Nyquist. It is interesting to note that Daniel Burke, Co-Director of the National Consortium on Options in Public Education, indicated his organization changed its name for much the same reason as Nyquist chose "optional learning environments" over "alternative schools." Burke said the old title, National Consortium on Educational Alternatives, was too easily confused with radical free schools. In order to draw the support of moderates within the public school system, the organization selected a more specific title. The phrase "educational alternatives" was considered too open to misinterpretation.
2. Otto F. Kraushaar, *American Nonpublic Schools: Patterns*

in Diversity (Baltimore: The Johns Hopkins University Press, 1972), pp. 16–17.

3. For a discussion of the "elitist" orientation of nonpublic alternative schools see the following works: E. Digby Baltzell, *Philadelphia Gentlemen: The Making of a National Upper Class* (Glencoe, Ill.: Free Press, 1958); C. Wright Mills, *The Power Elite* (New York: Oxford University Press, 1959); and Dixon Wecter, *The Saga of American Society: A Record of Social Aspiration: 1607–1937* (New York: C. Scribner's Sons, 1937).

4. Kraushaar, *American Nonpublic Schools*, p. 57.

5. Jon Whitney Wiles, "Southern Alternative Schools: A Portrait," *Educational Leadership*, vol. 29, no. 6 (March 1972), p. 537.

6. For a thorough description of the Summerhill philosophy see A. S. Neill, *Summerhill: A Radical Approach to Child Rearing* (New York: Hart, 1960).

7. Pauper schools and other nineteenth century alternatives are discussed by Michael B. Katz in *Class, Bureaucracy, & Schools: The Illusion of Educational Change in America* (New York: Praeger, 1971).

8. Robert D. Barr, "Whatever Happened to the Free School Movement?" in College of Continuing Education and the School of Education, University of Wisconsin—Oshkosh, *Education for a New Time* (n.c.: n.p., 1973), p. 164.

9. Harry S. Broudy, *The Real World of the Public Schools* (New York: Harcourt Brace Jovanovich, 1972), p 119.

10. *Changing Schools*, vol. 3: 4, no. 12 (1975).

11. Ewald B. Nyquist, "Optional Learning Environments," *Journal of the New York State School Boards Association, Inc.*, vol. 37, no. 3 (September 1973), p. 39.

12. Allen Graubard, *Free the Children: Radical Reform and the Free School Movement* (New York: Pantheon Books, 1973), pp. 40–41. Graubard's statistics seem to be confirmed by the publication "Free and Freedom Schools: A National Survey of Alternative Programs" (Washington, D. C.: President's Commission on School Finance, November 1971).

13. Kraushaar, *American Nonpublic Schools*, p. 17.

14. *Time*, April 26, 1971, p. 81.

15. For a discussion of recent revisionist works in educational history, see Maxine Greene, "Identities and Contours: An Approach to Educational History," *Educational Researcher,* vol. 2, no. 4 (April 1973), pp. 5–10.

16. In addition to corresponding with representatives of the National Association of Secondary School Principals, the National Association of Elementary School Principals, the National Consortium on Options in Public Education, and the National Alternative Schools Program, the author consulted the following published sources of alternative schools listings: Educational Research Service Circular Number 4, *Alternative High Schools: Some Pioneer Programs* (Washington, D. C.: Educational Research Service, 1972); "All about Alternatives," *Nation's Schools,* vol. 90 (November 1972), pp. 33–39; Allen C. Graubard, *New Schools: A National Directory of Alternative Schools* (n.c.: n.p., 1971); and *The New Schools Exchange Newsletter,* no. 81 (June 30, 1972). Other valuable listings were provided through the courtesy of Bonnie Beers of the Washington Area Free School Clearinghouse and Gordon Van Hooft, Acting Director of the Division of Secondary School Supervision, New York State Education Department.

17. There is no reason to expect a disproportionate number of alternative schools either east or west of the Mississippi. Graubard lists 186 out of 349 nonpublic alternatives east of the river. Of 47 public alternatives in the ERS circular, 24 are in this same region.

18. A complete list of the 40 schools in the sample can be found in the Addenda following Chapter 10.

19. Donald A. Myers and Daniel L. Duke, *Elementary School Appraisal—The Status of Open Education in New York State Public Elementary Schools, 1971–1972* (an unpublished research study completed under a State University of New York institutional grant in 1972).

20. For a detailed discussion of the importance of organizational structure in understanding the motives behind educational innovation, see Michael B. Katz's *Class, Bureaucracy, & Schools: The Illusion of Educational Change in America.* The same subject is addressed briefly in Robert Riordan's *Al-*

ternative Schools in Action (Bloomington, Ind.: Phi Delta Kappa Educational Foundation, 1972).

21. The importance of the social setting in which the school exists is stressed in the following works: Graubard's *Free the Children* and Jonathan Kozol's *Free Schools* (Boston: Houghton Mifflin, 1972).

22. For an analysis of contemporary alternative schools that focuses primarily on pedagogical dimensions, see the work of Richard W. Saxe, ed., *Opening the Schools: Alternative Ways of Learning* (Berkeley, Calif.: McCutchan, 1972).

23. Harold J. Leavitt, "Applied Organizational Change in Industry: Structural, Technological, and Humanistic Approaches," in James G. March (ed.), *Handbook of Organizations* (Chicago: Rand McNally, 1955), pp. 1144–1170.

24. For a copy of the final interview schedule used in the sample of 40 schools, see the Addenda following Chapter 10.

25. Anthony G. Oettinger, *Run, Computer, Run: The Mythology of Educational Innovation* (Cambridge: Harvard University Press, 1970), p. 60.

26. Graubard, *Free the Children*, p. 35.

27. For a detailed statement concerning traditional, nonquantitative trend analysis, see Wilhelm Dilthey, *Pattern and Meaning in History: Thoughts on History and Society* (New York: Harper & Row, 1962).

28. Joel H. Spring, *Education and the Rise of the Corporate State* (Boston: Beacon Press, 1972), p. 126.

29. Kraushaar, *American Nonpublic Schools*, p. 17.

30. For a discussion of organizational change and related ideas, see the following works: Warren G. Bennis, *Changing Organizations: Essays on the Development and Evolution of Human Organization* (New York: McGraw-Hill, 1966); Amitai Etzioni, *A Comparative Analysis of Complex Organizations: On Power, Involvement, and their Correlates* (New York: The Free Press of Glencoe, 1961); and Matthew Miles (ed.), *Innovation in Education* (New York: Teachers College Press, 1964).

31. Katz, *Class, Bureaucracy, & Schools*, p. 54.

32. Rosabeth Moss Kanter, *Commitment and Community: Com-*

munes and Utopias in Sociological Perspective (Cambridge: Harvard University Press, 1973), p. 62.

Chapter 2   Contemporary Alternative Schools: Their Goals

1. Allen Graubard, "The Free School Movement," *Harvard Educational Review*, vol. 42, no. 3 (August 1972), pp. 364–368.

2. Bruce S. Cooper, "Free and Freedom Schools: A National Survey of Alternative Programs" (Washington, D. C.: President's Commission on School Finance, November 1971).

3. See the brochure entitled "Alternative Education," published in 1972 by the Experimental Schools Program of the Berkeley Unified School District.

4. Broudy, *The Real World of the Public Schools*, p. 119.

5. Spring, *Education and the Rise of the Corporate State*, pp. 1–2.

6. Jonathan Kozol, "Free Schools: A Time for Candor," *Saturday Review*, March 1972, p. 54.

7. Graubard, *Free the Children*, p. 265.

8. Kanter, *Commitment and Community*, p. 166.

9. Winsor, *Experimental Schools Revisited*, p. 46.

10. Ibid.

11. Katz, *Class, Bureaucracy, & Schools*, p. 11.

12. Gerald L. Gutek, "New Harmony: An Example of Communitarian Education," *Educational Theory*, vol. 22, no. 1 (Winter 1972), p. 34.

13. For a brief discussion of the Organic School, refer to Lawrence Cremin's *The Transformation of the School*, pp. 147–153.

14. The Modern School is described by Joel Spring in *Education and the Rise of the Corporate State*, pp. 137–143. Manumit is discussed in the same book on pages 144–147.

15. Winsor, *Experimental Schools Revisited*, p. 69.

16. Kraushaar, *American Nonpublic Schools*, p. 78.

17. For a discussion of the Laboratory School, see Vynce A. Hines, "Progressivism in Practice," in *A New Look at Progressive Education*, ed. James R. Squire, pp. 118–164.

18. Philip Slater, *The Pursuit of Loneliness*.

Chapter 3   Contemporary Alternative Schools: Their Methods

1. Stephens, *The Process of Schooling*, p. 80.
2. This description was taken from a pamphlet entitled "Alternative Education," issued by the Seattle (Washington) Alternative Education Task Force.
3. "The Parkway Program" in *Opening the Schools: Alternative Ways of Learning*, ed. Richard W. Saxe, p. 300.
4. Cremin, *The Transformation of the School*, pp. 306–308.
5. Kraushaar, *American Nonpublic Schools*, p. 77.
6. Richard W. Saxe, "A Perspective on Alternatives," in *Opening the Schools*, ed. Richard W. Saxe, p. 396.

Chapter 4   Contemporary Alternative Schools: Their Administrative Organization

1. Katz, *Class, Bureaucracy, & Schools*, pp. 105–106.
2. Bonnie Barrett Stretch, "The Rise of the 'Free School,'" in *Schooling in a Corporate Society: The Political Economy of Education in America*, ed. Martin Carnoy, p. 211.
3. Sexton, *The American School*, p. 72.
4. Peter M. Blau, "Weber's Theory of Bureaucracy," in *Max Weber*, ed. Dennis Wrong, pp. 141–142.
5. Corwin, *A Sociology of Education*, p. 23.
6. Sloan R. Wayland, "The Teacher As Decision-Maker," in *Curriculum Crossroads*, ed. A. Harry Passow, p. 43.
7. The term "surrogate communes" is the suggestion of Professor Mauritz Johnson of the Department of Curriculum and Instruction at the State University of New York at Albany.
8. Kraushaar, *American Nonpublic Schools*, p. 265.
9. Ibid.
10. Ibid., pp. 267–268.
11. For a discussion of misconceptions concerning the rise of the American public school, see Colin Greer's *The Great School Legend: A Revisionist Interpretation of American Public Education*.
12. The author wishes to extend his appreciation for these ideas to Professor Arnold Foster of the Department of Sociology,

State University of New York at Albany.

13. Pratte, *The Public School Movement*, p. 56.
14. Katz, *Class, Bureaucracy, & Schools*, pp. 7–15.
15. Ibid., pp. 15–22.
16. Ibid., p. 17
17. Ibid., p. 39.
18. Ibid., p. 22
19. Pratte, *The Public School Movement*, p. 55.
20. Katz, *Class, Bureaucracy, & Schools*, p. 6.
21. Cronin, *The Control of Urban Schools*, p. 57.
22. Spring, *Education and the Rise of the Corporate State*, p. 148.
23. Ibid., p. 139.
24. John Dewey, *Democracy and Education* (New York: Free Press, 1966), pp. 98, 164, 358.
25. Broudy, *The Real World of the Public Schools*, p. 197.
26. Cremin, *The Transformation of the School*, p. 308.
27. Katz, *Class, Bureaucracy, & Schools*, p. 113.
28. Daniel C. Lortie, "The Cracked Cake of Educational Custom and Emerging Issues in Evaluation," in *Readings in Curriculum Evaluation*, eds. Peter A. Taylor and Doris M. Cowley, p. 67.
29. Spring, *Education and the Rise of the Corporate State,* p. 147.
30. Riordan, *Alternative Schools in Action*, p. 10.
31. The author was a participant in the convention and had an opportunity to discuss issues concerning contemporary alternative schools with many people active in the development of these schools.
32. Hodgkinson, *Education, Interaction, and Social Change*, p. 78.
33. Ibid.
34. For information on vouchers and related innovations, see David L. Kirp's "Vouchers, Reform, and the Elusive Community," *Teachers College Record*, vol. 74, no. 2 (December 1972), pp. 201–207.
35. Graubard, *Free the Children*, p. 36.
36. Marilyn R. Cohn and Mary Ellen Finch, "The Public Alternative High School: Solution to or Reflection of Societal Ills?" *Council on Anthropology and Education Quarterly*, vol. 6, no. 1 (February 1975), p. 14.

Chapter 5 Contemporary Alternative Schools: Their Composition

1. Leonard B. Finkelstein, "The Parkway Program Evaluation: The Director's Perspective," *Changing Schools*, no. 6, p. 17.
2. Giacquinta, "The Process of Organizational Change in Schools," p. 189.
3. Elizabeth Cleaners Street School, *Starting Your Own High School*, p. 3.
4. Graubard, *Free the Children*, p. 45.
5. Rotzel, *The School in Rose Valley*, p. 2.
6. Cremin, *The Transformation of the School*, p. 278.

Chapter 6 Impetus from the Top: The Conventional Origins of Contemporary Alternative Schools

1. Vernon H. Smith, "Alternative Public Schools: What Are They?" *NASSP Bulletin*, vol. 57, no. 374 (September 1973), pp. 4–6.
2. Kraushaar, *American Nonpublic Schools*, pp. 79–80.
3. Cremin, *The Transformation of the School*, p. 352.
4. Broudy, *The Real World of the Public Schools*, p. 20.
5. Ibid., pp. 20–21.
6 Cronin, *The Control of Urban Schools*, p. 181.
7. *Report of the National Advisory Commission on Civil Disorders*, p. 440.
8. Broudy, *The Real World of the Public Schools*, p. 13.
9. S. P. Marland, "Education and Public Confidence," *American Education*, vol. 9, no. 4 (May 1973), p. 6.
10. Broudy, *The Real World of the Public Schools*, p. 5.
11. James Q. Wilson and Robert L. DuPont, "The Sick Sixties," *The Atlantic Monthly*, vol. 232, no. 4 (October 1973), p. 95.
12 Ibid., p. 98.
13 John Geurnsey, "John Adams High School: Something for Everyone," in *High School*, eds. Ronald Gross and Paul Osterman, p. 270.
14. Riordan, *Alternative Schools in Action*, p. 11.
15. Ibid.
16. Bruce Howell, "Designing and Implementing Alternative

Schools," *NASSP Bulletin*, vol. 57, no. 374 (September 1973), p. 33.

17. Terry Borton, "Reform without Politics in Louisville," *Saturday Review*, February 5, 1972, p. 54.
18. *Educational Leadership*, vol. 29, no. 8 (May 1972), p. S–1.
19. For a detailed discussion of the origins of New York City's mini-schools, see Diane Divoky's "New York's Mini-Schools: Small Miracles, Big Troubles," *Saturday Review*, December 18, 1971, pp. 60–67.
20. Spring, *Education and the Rise of the Corporate State*, p. 137.
21. Riordan, *Alternative Schools in Action*, p. 32.
22. For a description of the first three ESP projects, see the publication by the U.S. Department of Health, Education, and Welfare/Office of Education, *Experimental Schools Program 1971*, p. 1.
23. For a discussion of recent national commissions concerned with educational innovation and alternative schools see Vernon H. Smith's "Alternative Public Schools: What Are They?" *NASSP Bulletin*, vol. 57, no. 374 (September 1973).
24. "News Exchange" (a newsletter published by the Association for Supervision and Curriculum Development), vol. 15, no. 4 (December 1973), p. 6.
25. Michael J. Bakalis, "A State Responds to Educational Need," *NASSP Bulletin*, vol. 57, no. 374 (September 1973), pp. 61–66.
26. Spring, *Education and the Rise of the Corporate State*, p. 149.
27. Broudy, *The Real World of the Public Schools*, p. 249.
28. For a provocative review of the events surrounding the International Convention on Options in Public Education see Dave Lehman's "Notes on How Not to Run an International Alternative Ed Convention," *The New Schools Exchange Newsletter*, no. 105, November 15, 1973, pp. 8–10. Lehman was one of the people involved in the floor critique of the convention's organizers.

Chapter 7   Impetus from Parents: The Grass-
roots Origins of Contemporary
Alternative Schools

1. Kozol, *Free Schools*, p. 1.

2. Robert D. Barr, "Whatever Happened to the Free School Movement!" in *Education of a New Time* (n.c.: n.p., 1973), College of Continuing Education and the School of Education, University of Wisconsin—Oshkosh, p. 162.

3. Graubard, *Free the Children*, p. xi.

4. Roszak, *The Making of a Counter Culture*, 1. 23.

5. Peter Schrag, "End of the Impossible Dream," *Saturday Review*, September 19, 1970, pp. 68–69.

6. Barth, *Open Education and the American School*, pp. 169–170.

7. S. P. Marland, "Education and Public Confidence," *American Education*, vol. 9, no. 4 (May 1973), p. 7.

8. Ibid., p. 6.

9. Broudy, *The Real World of the Public Schools*, p. 89.

10. Jerome T. Murphy, "Title V of ESEA: The Impact of Discretionary Funds on State Education Bureaucracies," *Harvard Educational Review*, vol. 43, no. 3 (August 1973), p. 385.

11. Hofstadter, *The Age of Reform*, p. 135.

12. Ibid., p. 216.

13. Ibid., p. 217.

14. According to Lewis S. Feuer, in *The Conflict of Generations* (p. 407), the term "participatory democracy" was introduced into radical parlance as a result of the Port Huron gathering in 1962 that witnessed the creation of Students for a Democratic Society.

15. Hofstadter, *The Age of Reform*, p. 269.

16. For a detailed account of radical activism in the thirties, see Lewis S. Feuer's *The Conflict of Generations: The Character and Significance of Student Movements*.

17. James Q. Wilson and Robert L. DuPont, "The Sick Sixties," *The Atlantic Monthly*, vol. 232, no. 4 (October 1973), p. 95.

18. Kenneth Keniston, "Beyond Technology," in *In Pursuit of Awareness: The College Student in the Modern World*, eds. Esther Kronovet and Evelyn Shirk, p. 555.

19. Two examples of these critical works are Edgar Z. Friedenberg, *Coming of Age in America: Growth and Acquiescence*, and Paul Goodman, *Compulsory Mis-Education and the Community of Scholars*.

20. For a review of Weber's thinking, see Dennis Wrong's *Max Weber*.

21. Maxine Greene, "Identities and Contours: An Approach to Educational History," *Educational Researcher,* vol. 2, no. 4 (April 1973), p. 7.
22. Roszak, *The Making of a Counter Culture,* pp. 6–7.
23. Ibid., p. 7.
24. Zijderveld, *The Abstract Society,* p. 128.
25. Marland, "Education and Public Confidence," p. 8.
26. Slater, *The Pursuit of Loneliness,* p. 140.
27. Alvin Toffler, "Education in the Future Tense," in *Opening the Schools: Alternative Ways of Learning,* ed. Richard W. Saxe, p. 3.
28. James J. Morisseau, "A Conversation with Alvin Toffler, *The National Elementary Principal,* vol. 52, no. 4 (January 1973), p. 14.
29. Henry Levin, "The Case for Community Control of Schools," in *Schooling in a Corporate Society: The Political Economy of Education in America,* ed. Martin Carnoy, 1. 195.
30. Albert Shanker, "Cult of Localism," in *School Policy and Issues in a Changing Society,* ed. Patricia C. Sexton, p. 219.
31. Levin, "The Case for Community Control of Schools," p. 204.
32. Kanter, *Commitment and Community,* p. 7.
33. The quote comes from a pamphlet entitled "A Realistic Alternative: Thurana School," which is distributed by members of the school.
34. Larry Olds, "Notes on the Community School," in *Education Explorer: A Look at New Learning Spaces,* Education Exploration Center, pages unnumbered.
35. Kozol, *Free Schools,* p. 22.
36. Broudy, *The Real World of the Public Schools,* p. 10.
37. Colette Dowling, "What Will Happen to the Children?" *Saturday Review,* October 14, 1972, p. 49.
38. Powers, *Diana: The Making of a Terrorist,* p. 65.
39. Katz, *Class, Bureaucracy, & Schools,* p. 3.

Chapter 8 Impetus from Students: The Grass-roots Origins of Contemporary Alternative Schools

1. Pratte, *The Public School Movement,* pp. 174–175.
2. Bremer and von Moschzisker, *The School without Walls, p.

133.

3. Slater, *The Pursuit of Loneliness*, p. 122.
4. Feuer, *The Conflict of Generations*, p. 507.
5. Williams, *American Society: A Sociological Interpretation*, p. 348.
6. Flacks, *Youth and Social Change*, p. 45.
7. Robert Jay Lifton, "Individual Patterns in Historical Change: Imagery of Japanese Youth," in *Personality and Social Systems*, eds. Neil J. Smelser and William T. Smelser, p. 551.
8. Larry Wells, "Options in a Small District: Berkeley," *NASSP Bulletin*, vol. 57, no. 374 (September 1973), p. 56.

Chapter 9 Impetus from Teachers: The Grass-roots Origins of Contemporary Alternative Schools

1. Sloan R. Wayland, "Structural Features of American Education as Basic Factors in Innovation," in *Innovation in Education*, ed. Matthew Miles, p. 612.
2. Wayland, "The Teacher as Decision-Maker," p. 48.
3. Connie Donofrio and Ruth Katz, "Bethlehem Community School," in *Education Explorer: A Look at New Learning Spaces*, pages unnumbered.
4. Kozol, *Free Schools*, pp. 14–15.

Chapter 10 The Retransformation of the School

1. Broudy, *The Real World of the Public Schools*, p. 148.
2. Harry S. Broudy and John R. Palmer, *Exemplars of Teaching Method* (Chicago: Rand McNally, 1970), p. 160.
3. Jim Warren, "Alum Rock Voucher Project," *Educational Researcher*, vol. 5, no. 3 (March 1976), p. 14.
4. Ibid., p. 15
5 For a discussion of current interests among Chicano educators, see the Southwest Network of the Study Commission on Undergraduate Education and the Education of Teachers, *Chicano Alternative Education* (n.c.: n.p., n.d.). The book may be ordered from the Southwest Network, 1020 B Street, Hayward, California 94541
6. Lawrence Kohlberg, "The Cognitive-Developmental Approach

to Moral Education," *Phi Delta Kappan*, vol. 56, no. 10 (June 1975), p. 676.

7. A. Harry Passow, "Reforming America's High Schools," *Phi Delta Kappan*, vol. 56, no. 9 (May 1975), p. 588.

8. See the following research studies: Chris Argyris, "Alternative Schools: A Behavioral Analysis," *Teachers College Record*, vol. 75, no. 4 (May 1974), pp. 429–452; Bruce S. Cooper, "Organizational Survival: A Comparative Case Study of Seven American "Free Schools," *Education and Urban Society*, vol. 5, no. 4 (August 1973), pp. 487–508; Terrence E. Deal, "An Organizational Explanation of the Failure of Alternative Secondary Schools," *Educational Researcher*, vol. 4, no. 4 (April 1975), pp. 10–16; and Steven Singleton, et al., "Xanadu: A Study of the Structure Crisis in an Alternative School." *Review of Educational Research*, vol. 42, no. 4 (Fall 1972), pp. 525–531.

9. Refer to the study by A. J. H. Gaite and Richard J. Rankin, Patterns of Achievement, Attitude, and Behavior in a Tax-Supported Alternative School," *Journal of Experimental Education*, vol. 43, no. 3 (Spring 1975), pp. 35–39.

10. Ralph T. Nelsen, "FOCUS: An Alternative Model That Works," *Phi Delta Kappan*, vol. 56, no. 9 (May 1975), p. 631.

11. Refer to evaluation summaries by Edsel L. Erickson, et al., *The Southeast Community Education Center. Final Evaluation Report* (Kalamazoo, Michigan: Information Services, Inc., 1975) and Michael H. Walizer, et al., *Madison Park Alternative Education Program: Sweet Street Academy. Final Evaluation Report* (Kalamazoo, Michigan: Information Services, 1975).

12. Warren, "Alum Rock Voucher Project," p. 14.

13. Riordan, *Alternative Schools in Action*, p. 45.

Bibliography

I. SOURCES DEALING SPECIFICALLY WITH ALTERNATIVES

Aldrich, Ruth Anne. *Marcy Open School: 1973-1974. Goal Evaluation* (Minneapolis: Minneapolis Public Schools, 1974).

Areen, Judith C. "Alternative Schools: Better Guardians Than Family or State?" *School Review*, vol. 81, no. 2 (February 1973), pp. 175-193.

Argyris, Chris. "Alternative Schools: A Behavorial Analysis," *Teachers College Record*, vol. 75, no. 4 (May 1974), pp. 429-452.

Barr, Robert D. "The Growth of Alternative Public Schools: The 1975 ICOPE Report," *Changing Schools*, vol. 3:4, no. 12 (1975).

Barth, Roland S. *Open Education and the American School* (New York: Agathon Press, 1972).

_____. "Should We Forget about Open Education?" *Saturday Review/World*, (November 6, 1973), pp. 58–59.

Bennett, Harold Zina. *No More Public School* (New York: Random House, 1972).

Bhaerman, Steve and Joel Denker. *No Particular Place to Go: The Making of a Free High School* (New York: Simon and Schuster, 1972).

Boskind-Ginsburg, Marlene. "East Hill School—The Story of an Innovation" (unpublished essay, 1971).

Bremer, John and Michael von Moschzisker. *The School without Walls: Philadelphia's Parkway Program* (New York: Holt, Rinehart and Winston, 1971).

Brownson, Bill. "Alternative Schools and the Problem of Change: School Is a School Is a School Is a School," *Contemporary Education*, vol. 44, no. 5 (April 1973), pp. 298–303.

Center for New Schools. "Decision-Making in Alternative Secondary Schools: Report from a National Conference, May 25, 1972" (Chicago: Center for New Schools, 1972).

_____. "Strengthening Alternative High Schools," *Harvard Educational Review*, vol. 42, no. 3 (August 1972), pp. 313–350.

Closson, B. Michael, Richard Harris, and Frederick Stutz. "Trials of an Experimental Public School" (unpublished essay, 1971).

Cohn, Marilyn R. and Mary Ellen Finch. "The Public Alternative High School: Solution to or Reflection of Societal Ills?" *Council on Anthropology and Education Quarterly*, vol. 6, no. 1 (February 1975), pp. 9–15.

Cooper, Bruce S. "Free and Freedom Schools: A National Survey of Alternative Programs" (Washington, D.C.: President's Commission on School Finance, November 1971).

_____. "Organizational Survival: A Comparative Case Study of Seven American 'Free Schools,'" *Education and Urban Society*, vol. 5, no. 4 (August 1973), pp. 487–508.

Crabtree, Mary Francis. "Chicago's Metro High: Freedom, Choice, Responsibility," *Phi Delta Kappan*, vol. 56, no. 9 (May 1975), pp. 613–615.

Davis, Barbara Gross. "Evaluating Innovative Programs: The Berkeley Perspective" (paper presented for the 1976 AERA Symposium Presentation: Internal Evaluation in the Experimental Schools Projects).

Deal, Terrence E. "An Organizational Explanation of the Failure of Alternative Secondary Schools," *Educational Researcher*, vol. 4, no. 4 (April 1975), pp. 10–16.

Dennison, George. *The Lives of Children: The Story of the First Street School* (New York: Random House, 1969).

DeTurk, Philip and Robert Mackin. "Lions in the Park: An Alternative Meaning and Setting for Learning," *Phi Delta Kappan,* vol. 54, no. 7 (March 1973), pp. 458–460.

Dewey, John and Evelyn Dewey. *Schools of Tomorrow* (New York: Dutton, 1962).

Divoky, Diane. "Berkeley's Experimental Schools," *Saturday Review* (September 16, 1972), pp. 44–51.

————. "New York's Mini-Schools: Small Miracles, Big Troubles," *Saturday Review* (December 18, 1971), pp. 60–67.

————. "Young Ideas in an Old State," *Saturday Review* (April 18, 1970), pp. 62–78.

Duke, Daniel Linden. "Alternative Schools," in Donald A. and Lilian Myers (eds.), *Open Education Re-Examined* (Lexington, Mass.: Lexington Books, 1973), pp. 65–85.

————. "Beyond Curriculum and Instruction: Alternative Schools and Organizational Revolution" (unpublished essay, 1973).

————. "Challenge to Bureaucracy: The Contemporary Alternative School," *The Journal of Educational Thought,* vol. 1, no. 1 (April 1976) pp. 34–48.

————. "Decision-Making in the Alternative School" (unpublished essay, 1972).

Duke, Daniel Linden and Irene Muzio. "How Effective Are Alternative Schools?—A Review of Recent Evaluations and Reports" (in press).

Education Exploration Center. *Education Explorer: A Look at New Learning Spaces* (Minneapolis: Education Exploration Center, 1971).

Educational Research Service. *Alternative High Schools: Some Pioneer Programs* (Washington, D.C.: Educational Research Service, 1972).

Elizabeth Cleaners Street School. *Starting Your Own High School* (New York: Vintage Books, 1972).

Erickson, Edsel L. et al. *The Southeast Community Education Center. Final Evaluation Report* (Kalamazoo, Mich.: Information Services, 1975).

Experimental Schools Program. "Alternative Education" (Berkeley: Experimental Schools Program, October 1972).

Fantini, Mario D. "Alternatives within Public Schools," *Phi Delta Kappan,* vol. 54, no. 7 (March 1973), pp. 444–448.

————. "Education by Choice," *NASSP Bulletin,* vol. 57, no. 374 (September 1973), pp. 10–19.

————. *Public Schools of Choice* (New York: Simon and Schuster, 1973).

————. "Testing Time," *Saturday Review of Education* (March 1973), pp. 69–70.

Finkelstein, Leonard B. "The Parkway Program Evaluation: The Director's Perspective," *Changing Schools,* no. 6, pp. 16–19.

Gaite, A. J. H. and Richard J. Rankin "Patterns of Achievement Attitude, and Behavior in a Tax-Supported Alternative School," *Journal of Experimental Education,* vol. 43, no. 3 (Spring 1975), pp. 35–39.

Geurnsey, John. "John Adams High School: Something for Everyone," in Ronald Gross and Paul Osterman (eds.), *High School* (New York: Simon and Schuster, 1971), pp. 263–271.

Glick, Oren. Untitled paper presented for distribution in conjunction with the 1976 AERA Symposium Presentation: Internal Evaluation in the Experimental Schools Projects 1976.

Graubard, Allen. "The Free School Movement," *Harvard Educational Review,* vol. 42, no. 3 (August 1972), pp. 351–373.

————. *Free the Children: Radical Reform and the Free School Movement* (New York: Pantheon, 1973).

————. *New Schools: A National Directory of Alternative Schools* (n.c.: n.p., 1971).

Greeley, Andrew M. "Public and Nonpublic Schools—Losers Both," *School Review,* vol. 81, no. 2 (February 1973), pp. 195–206.

Gross, Ronald. "From Innovations to Alternatives: A Decade of Change in Education," *Phi Delta Kappan,* vol. 53, no. 6 (September, 1971), pp. 22–24.

Gutek, Gerald L. "New Harmony: An Example of Communitarian Education," *Educational Theory,* vol. 22, no. 1 (Winter 1972), pp. 34–46.

Hines, Vynce A. "Progressivism in Practice," in James R. Squire (ed.); *A New Look at Progressive Education* (Washington,

D.C.: Association for Supervision and Curriculum Development, 1972), pp. 118–164.

Howell, Bruce. "Designing and Implementing Alternative Schools," *NASSP Bulletin*, vol. 57, no. 374 (September 1973), pp. 32–38.

Jacoby, Susan. "What Happened When a High School Tried Self-Government," *Saturday Review* (April 1, 1973), pp. 49–53.

Johnson, David L. and Jackson V. Parker, "Walden III: The Alternative High School Survives Evaluation Quite Nicely, Thank You," *Phi Delta Kappan*, vol. 56, no. 9 (May 1975), p. 625.

Katz, Michael B. *Class, Bureaucracy, & Schools: The Illusion of Educational Change in America* (New York: Praeger, 1971).

————. (ed.) *School Reform: Past and Present* (Boston: Little, Brown, 1971).

Kaye, Michael S. *The Teacher Was the Sea: The Story of Pacific High School* (New York: Links Books, 1972).

Kirp, David L. "Vouchers, Reform, and the Elusive Community," *Teachers College Record*, vol. 74, no. 2 (December 1972), pp. 201–207.

Kocher, A. Thel. "Evaluating Innovative Programs: The Minneapolis Perspective" (paper prepared for the 1976 AERA Symposium Presentation: Internal Evaluation in the Experimental Schools Projects).

Kohlberg, Lawrence. "The Cognitive-Developmental Approach to Moral Education," *Phi Delta Kappan*, vol. 56, no. 10 (June 1975), pp. 670–677.

Kozol, Jonathan. *Free Schools* (Boston: Houghton Mifflin, 1972).

————. "Free Schools: A Time for Candor," *Saturday Review* (March 4, 1972), pp. 51–54.

————. "Moving On—To Nowhere," *Saturday Review* (December 9, 1972), pp. 6–14.

Kraushaar, Otto F. *American Nonpublic Schools: Patterns of Diversity* (Baltimore: The Johns Hopkins University Press, 1972).

Kritek, William J. "The Design and Implementation of an Alternative High School" (paper presented at AERA annual meeting, April 22, 1976).

Love, Robert. *How to Start Your Own School: A Guide for the Radical Right, the Radical Left, and Everybody In-Between*

Who's Fed Up with Public Education (New York: Macmillan, 1973).

McCauley, B. L., S. M. Dornbusch, and W. Scott. "Evaluation and Authority in Alternative Schools and Public Schools" Stanford Center for Research and Development in Teaching Technical Report No. 23 (Stanford: Stanford Center for Research and Development in Teaching, 1972).

McLachlan, James. *American Boarding Schools: A Historical Study* (New York: Charles Scribner's Sons, 1970).

Marin, Peter. "Has Imagination Outstripped Reality?" *Saturday Review* (July 22, 1972), pp. 40–44.

Moore, Donald R., Thomas A. Wilson, and Richard Johnson. *The Metro School: A Report on the Progress of Chicago's Experimental "School without Walls"* (Chicago: Urban Research Corporation, 1971).

Moss, Jeanette K. "Alternatives: 4 Schools of Choice," *Teacher*, vol. 91, no. 5 (January 1974), pp. 33–37.

Myers, Donald A. and Daniel L. Duke. *Elementary School Appraisal—The Status of Open Education in New York State Public Elementary Schools, 1971–72* (unpublished research study completed under the auspices of a State University of New York at Albany institutional grant).

Nation's Schools. "All about Alternatives," vol. 90, no. 5 (November 1972), pp. 33–39.

Neill, A. S. *Summerhill: A Radical Approach to Child Rearing* (New York: Hart, 1960).

Nelsen, Ralph T. "FOCUS: An Alternative Model That Works," *Phi Delta Kappan*, vol. 56, no. 9 (May 1975), p. 631.

Nyquist, Ewald B. "Optional Learning Environments," *Journal of the New York State School Boards Association, Inc.*, vol. 37, no. 3 (September 1973), pp. 36–40.

Passow, A. Harry. "Reforming America's High Schools," *Phi Delta Kappan*, vol. 56, no. 9 (May 1975), pp. 587–590.

Patenade, John and Marge Hart. "Demythicizing Movements," *The New Schools Exchange Newsletter*, no. 85 (October 31, 1972), pp. 2–3.

Powers, Thomas. *Diana: The Making of a Terrorist* (Boston: Houghton Mifflin, 1971).

Rasberry, Salli and Robert Greenway. *Rasberry Exercises* (Freestone, Calif.: Freestone, 1971).

Rathbone, Charles H. "Examining the Open Education Classroom," *School Review*, vol. 80, no. 4 (August 1972), pp. 521–549.

Reeves, Patricia. *Southeast Alternatives Free School End of Year Report* (Minneapolis: Minneapolis Public Schools, 1974).

Reimer, Everett. *An Essay on Alternatives in Education* (Cuernavaca, Mexico: CIDOC, 1970).

――――. *School Is Dead: Alternatives in Education* (Garden City, N.Y. Doubleday, 1971).

Repo, Satu (ed.). *This Book Is about Schools* (New York: Vintage Books, 1970).

Riordan, Robert C. *Alternative Schools in Action* (Bloomington, Ind.: Phi Delta Kappan Educational Foundation, 1972).

Rosen, David, J. and Gene Mulcahy. "Evaluation—Shanti: A Case Study," *Changing Schools*, vol. 4:2, no. 14 (1975).

Rotzel, Grace. *The School in Rose Valley: A Parent Venture in Education* (New York: Ballantine, 1972).

Rusk, Bruce (ed.). *Alternatives in Education: OISE Fifth Anniversary Lectures* (Toronto: General Publishing Company Limited, 1971).

Saxe, Richard W. (ed.). *Opening the Schools: Alternative Ways of Learning* (Berkeley: McCutchan, 1972).

Simon, Robert I., et al. *The Development and Evaluation of an Alternative High School: A Report on S.E.E. (School of Experimental Education), Phase 2* (Toronto: Ontario Institute for Studies in Education, 1973).

Singleton, Steven, David Boyer, and Paul Dorsey. "Xandau: A Study of the Structure Crisis in an Alternative School," *Review of Educational Research*, vol. 42, no. 4 (Fall 1972), pp. 525–531.

Sizer, Theodore R. *The Age of the Academies* (New York: Bureau of Publications, Teachers College, Columbia University, 1964).

Skutch, Margaret and Wilfred G. Hamlin. *To Start a School* (Boston: Little, Brown, 1971).

Smith, Vernon H. "Alternative Public Schools: What Are They?" *NASSP Bulletin*, vol. 57, no. 374 (September 1973), pp. 4–9.

――――. "Options in Public Education: The Quiet Revolution," *Phi Delta Kappan*, vol. 54, no. 7 (March 1973), pp. 434–437.

Southwest Network of the Study Commission on Undergraduate

Education and the Education of Teachers. *Casa de la Raza* (n.c.: n.p., n.d.) Southwest Network, 1020 B Street, Hayward, Calif, 94541.

_____. *Chicano Alternative Education* (n.c.: n.p., n.d.)

Tucker, Gilbert M. *The Private School: Its Advantages, Its Problems, Its Financing* (New York: Vintage Press, 1965).

U.S. Department of Health, Education and Welfare/Office of Education. *Experimental Schools Program 1971* (Washington, D.C.: U. S. Government Printing Office, 1971).

Walizer, Michael H., et al. *Madison Park Alternative Education Program: Sweet Street Academy. Final Evaluation Report* (Kalamazoo, Mich.: Information Services, Inc., 1975).

Warren, Jim. "Alum Rock Voucher Project," *Educational Researcher*, vol. 5, no. 3 (March 1976), pp. 13–15.

Wells, Larry. "Options in a Small District: Berkeley," *NASSP Bulletin*, vol. 57, no. 374 (September 1973), pp. 55–60.

Wiles, Jon Whitney. "Southern Alternative Schools: A Portrait," *Educational Leadership*, vol. 29, no. 6 (March 1972), pp. 534–538.

Winsor, Charlotte (ed.). *Experimental Schools Revisited: Bulletins of the Bureau of Educational Experiments* (New York: Agathon Press, 1973).

II. GENERAL EDUCATIONAL REFERENCES

Adams, Don. *Schooling and Social Change in Modern America* (New York: David McKay, 1972).

Anderson, Barry D. and Holden Baker. "Status Differences in Schools," *Teachers College Record*, vol. 73, no. 4 (May 1972), pp. 567–576.

Anderson, James C. "The Authority Structure of the School: System of Social Exchange." *Educational Administration Quarterly*, vol. 3, no. 2 (Spring 1967), pp. 130–148.

Bakalis, Michael J. "A State Responds to Educational Need," *NASSP Bulletin*, vol. 57, no. 374 (September 1973), pp. 61–66.

Banks, Olive. *The Sociology of Education* (New York: Schocken Books, 1972).

Bereiter, Carl. "Schools without Education." *Harvard Educational Review*, vol. 42, no. 3 (August 1972), pp. 390–413.

Bidwell, Charles E. "The School as a Formal Organization," in James G. March (ed.), *Handbook of Organizations* (Chicago: Rand McNally, 1965), pp. 972–1022.

Birmingham, John (ed.). *Our Time Is Now: Notes from the High School Underground* (New York: Praeger, 1970).

Borton, Terry. "Reform without Politics in Louisville." *Saturday Review* (February 5, 1972), pp. 50–55.

Broudy, Harry. *The Real World of the Public Schools* (New York: Harcourt Brace Jovanovich, 1972).

Broudy, Harry S. and John R. Palmer, *Exemplars of Teaching Method.* (Chicago: Rand McNally, 1970).

Bussis, Anne M. and Edward A. Chittenden. *Analysis of an Approach to Open Education* (Princeton, N. J.: Educational Testing Service, 1970).

Carnoy, Martin. *Schooling in a Corporate Society: The Political Economy of Education in America* (New York: David McKay Company, Inc., 1972).

College of Continuing Education and the School of Education, University of Wisconsin—Oshkosh. *Education for a New Time* (n.c.: n.p., 1973).

Corwin, Ronald G. *A Sociology of Education: Emerging Patterns of Class, Status, and Power in the Public Schools* (New York: Appleton-Century-Crofts, 1965).

Cremin, Lawrence A. *The Transformation of the Schools: Progressivism in American Education, 1876–1957* (New York: Random House, 1964).

Cronin, Joseph M. *The Control of Urban Schools: Perspective on the Power of Educational Reformers* (New York: The Free Press, 1973).

Dowling, Colette, "What Will Happen to the Children." *Saturday Review* (October 14, 1972), pp. 45–49.

Getzels, Jacob W. "Administration as a Social Process," in Andrew W. Halpin (ed.), *Administrative Theory in Education* (Chicago: Midwest Administration Center, 1958), pp. 150–165.

Goodman, Paul. *Compulsory Mis-Education and the Community of Scholars* (New York: Vintage Books, 1964).

Greene, Maxine. "Identities and Contours: An Approach to Educational History." *Educational Researcher,* vol. 2, no. 4 (April 1973), pp. 5–10.

Greer, Colin. *The Great School Legend: A Revisionist Interpretation of American Public Education* (New York: Basic Books, 1972).

Griffiths, Daniel E. "Administration as Decision-Making," in Andres W. Halpin (ed.), *Administrative Theory in Education* (Chicago: Midwest Administration Center, 1958), pp. 119–149.

Guthrie, James W. and Paula H. Skene. "The Escalation of Pedagogical Politics," *Phi Delta Kappan*, vol. 54, no. 6 (February 1973), pp. 386–389.

Hein, Margaret Gill. "Planning and Organizing for Improved Instruction," in William J. Ellena (ed.), *Curriculum Handbook for School Executives* (Arlington, Va.: American Association of School Administrators, 1973), pp. 365–379.

Jencks, Christopher, et al. *Inequality* (New York: Harper Colophon Books, 1972).

Kerlinger, Fred N. (ed.). *Review of Research in Education: I* (Itasca, Ill.: Peacock, 1973).

Kozol, Jonathan. *Death at an Early Age* (New York: Bantam Books, Inc., 1967).

Lortie, Daniel C. "The Cracked Cake of Educational Custom and Emerging Issues in Evaluation," in Peter A. Taylor and Doris M. Cowley (eds.), *Readings in Curriculum Evaluation* (Dubuque, Iowa: Wm. C. Brown, 1972), pp. 64–72.

Maryland, S. P. "Education and Public Confidence," *American Education*, vol 9, no. 4 (May 1973), pp. 5–10.

Mayer, Martin. *The Schools* (New York: Harper & Brothers, 1961).

Miles, Matthew (ed.). *Innovation in Education* (New York: Teachers College Press, 1964).

Murphy, Jerome T. "Title V of ESEA: The Impact of Discretionary Funds on State Education Bureaucracies," *Harvard Educational Review*, vol. 43, no. 3 (August 1973), pp. 362–385.

Oettinger, Anthony G. *Run, Computer, Run: The Mythology of Educational Innovation* (Cambridge: Harvard University Press, 1970).

Pratte, Richard. *The Public School Movement* (New York: David McKay, 1973).

Rosenthal, Alan (ed.). *Governing Education: A Reader of Pol-*

itics, Power, and Public School Policy (Garden City, N. Y.: Anchor Books, 1969).

Sarason, Seymour B. *The Culture of the School and the Problem of Change* (Boston: Allyn and Bacon, 1971).

Selakovich, Daniel. *The Schools and American Society* (Waltham, Mass.: Blaisdell, 1967).

Sexton, Patricia Cayo. *The American School: A Sociological Analysis* (Englewood Cliffs, N. J.: Prentice-Hall, 1967).

————. (ed.). *School Policy and Issues in a Changing Society* (Boston: Allyn and Bacon, 1971).

Silberman, Charles E. *Crisis in the Classroom: The Remaking of American Education* (New York: Random House, 1970).

Spring, Joel. *Education and the Rise of the Corporate State* (Boston: Beacon Press, 1972).

Stephens, J. M. *The Process of Schooling: A Psychological Examination* (New York: Holt, Rinehart and Winston, 1967).

Wayland, Sloan R. "The Teacher as Decision-Maker," in A. Harry Passow (ed.), *Curriculum Crossroads* (New York: Bureau of Publications, Teachers College, Columbia University, 1962), pp. 41–52.

Ylvisaker, Paul N. "Beyond '72: Strategies for Schools," *Saturday Review* (November 11, 1972), pp. 33–34.

III. SOCIAL SCIENCE AND THEORETICAL RESOURCES

Ash, Roberta T. "Durkheim's *Moral Education* Reconsidered: Toward the Creation of a Counterculture," *School Review*, vol. 80, no. 1 (November 1971), pp. 111–142.

Baltzell, E. Digby. *Philadelphia Gentlemen: The Making of a National Upper Class* (Glencoe, Ill.: Free Press, 1958).

Bennis, Warren G. *Changing Organizations: Essays on the Development and Evolution of Human Organization* (New York: McGraw-Hill, 1966).

Bennis, Warren G. and Philip E. Slater. *The Temporary Society* (New York: Harper & Row, 1969).

Bernstein, Barton J. (ed.). *Towards a New Past: Dissenting Essays in American History* (New York: Vintage Books, 1969).

Blau, Peter M. "Weber's Theory of Bureaucracy," in Dennis

Wrong (ed.), *Max Weber* (Englewood Cliffs, N. J.: Prentice-Hall, 1970), pp. 141–145.

Boguslaw, Robert. *The New Utopians: A Study of System Design and Social Change* (Englewood Cliffs, N.J.: Prentice-Hall, 1965).

Crozier, Michel. *The Bureaucratic Phenomenon* (Chicago: The University of Chicago Press, 1967).

Dilthey, Wilhelm. *Pattern and Meaning in History: Thoughts on History and Society* (New York: Harper & Row, 1962).

Etzioni, Amitai. *A Comparative Anlysis of Complex Organizations: On Power, Involvement, and Their Correlates* (New York: The Free Press of Glencoe, 1961).

————. "Human Beings Are Not Very Easy to Change after All," *Saturday Review* (June 3, 1972), pp. 45–47.

————. *Modern Organizations* (Englewood Cliffs N. J.: Prentice-Hall, 1964).

Feuer, Lewis S. *The Conflict of Generations: The Character and Significance of Student Movements* (New York: Basic Books, 1969).

Flacks, Richard. *Youth and Social Change* (Chicago: Markham, 1972).

Friedenberg, Edgar Z. *Coming of Age in America: Growth and Acquiescence* (New York: Vintage Books, 1965).

Hodgkinson, Harold L. *Education, Interaction, and Social Change* (Englewood Cliffs, N. J.: Prentice-Hall, 1967).

Hofstadter, Richard. *The Age of Reform* (New York: Vintage Books, 1955).

Kanter, Rosabeth Moss. *Commitment and Community: Communes and Utopias in Sociological Perspective* (Cambridge, Mass.: Harvard University Press, 1973).

Keniston, Kenneth. "The Agony of the Counter-Culture," *Yale Alumni Magazine,* vol. 35, no. 1 (October 1971), pp. 10–13.

Kronovet, Esther and Evelyn Shirk. *In Pursuit of Awareness: The College Student in the Modern World* (New York: Appleton-Century-Crofts, 1967).

Leavitt, Harold J. "Applied Organizational Change in Industry: Structural, Technological, and Humanistic Approaches," in James G. March (ed.), *Handbook of Organizations* (Chicago: Rand McNally, 1965), pp. 1144–1170.

Lenski, Gerhard. *Power and Privilege: A Theory of Social Stratification* (New York: McGraw-Hill, 1966).

LeVine, Robert A. *Culture, Behavior, and Personality* (Chicago: Aldine, 1973).

Lewis, Anthony and *The New York Times. Portrait of a Decade: The Second Revolution* (New York: Bantam Books, 1971).

Lynd, Staughton. *Intellectual Origins of American Radicalism* (New York: Vintage Books, 1969).

Meadows, Paul. *The Many Faces of Change: Explorations in the Theory of Social Change* (Cambridge: Schenkman, 1971).

Melville, Keith. *Communes in the Counter Culture: Origins, Theories, Styles of Life* (New York: William Morrow, 1972).

Mills, C. Wright. *The Power Elite* (New York: Oxford University Press, 1959).

Morisseau, James J. "A Conversation with Alvin Toffler," *The National Elementary Principal,* vol. 52, no. 4 (January 1973), pp. 8–18.

Muller, Herbert J. *The Children of Frankenstein: A Primer on Modern Technology and Human Values* (Bloomington, Ind.: Indiana University Press, 1970).

Nisbet, Robert A. *The Quest for Community* (London: Oxford University Press, 1971).

Packard, Vance. *A Nation of Strangers* (New York: David McKay, 1972).

Report of the National Advisory Commission on Civil Disorders (New York: Bantam Books, 1968).

Roszak, Theodore. *The Making of a Counter Culture: Reflections on the Technocratic Society and Its Youthful Opposition* (Garden City, N. Y.: Doubleday, 1969).

————. *Where the Wasteland Ends: Politics and Transcendence in Postindustrial Society* (Garden City, N. Y.: Doubleday, 1972).

Ruitenbeek, Hendrik M. (ed.). *Varieties of Modern Social Theory* (New York: Dutton, 1963).

Ryan, William. *Blaming the Victim* (New York: Pantheon Books, 1971).

Schrag, Peter. "End of the Impossible Dream," *Saturday Review* (September 19, 1970), pp. 68–69.

Seeman, Melvin. "On the Meaning of Alienation," *American Sociological Review,* vol. 24 (December 1959), pp. 783–791.

Slater, Philip. *The Pursuit of Loneliness: American Culture at the Breaking Point* (Boston: Beacon Press, 1971).

Smelser, Neil J. and William T. Smelser (eds.). *Personality and Social Systems* (New York: Wiley, 1970).

Toffler, Alvin. *Future Shock* (New York: Bantam Books, 1971).

Wax, Murray L., Stanley Diamond, and Fred O. Gearing (eds.) *Anthropological Perspectives on Education* (New York: Basic Books, 1971).

Wecter, Dixon. *The Saga of American Society: A Record of Social Aspiration, 1607–1937* (New York: C. Scribner's Sons, 1937).

Williams, Robin M., Jr. *American Society: A Sociological Interpretation* (New York: Knopf, 1970).

Wilson, James Q. and Robert L. DuPont. "The Sick Sixties," *The Atlantic Monthly,* vol. 232, no. 4 (October 1973), pp. 91–98.

Yankelovich, Daniel "The New Naturalism," *Saturday Review* (April 1, 1972), pp. 32–37.

Zijderveld, Anton C. *The Abstract Society: A Cultural Analysis of Our Time* (Garden City, N. Y.: Anchor, 1971).

Index

CENTRAL COLLEGE LIBRARY
PELLA, IOWA 50219

About the Author

DANIEL LINDEN DUKE is a professor at Stanford University's School of Education. He holds a B.A. from Yale University, a Ed.D. from the State University of New York at Albany and is himself the cofounder of an alternative school. His professional contributions include two chapters on alternative schools and open education in *Open Education Re-Examined* (Donald and Lilian Myers, editors), and articles in the Journal of *Educational Thought, SAANYS Journal,* and *Educational Digest.*